I0216273

Karmic Astrology

The Ultimate Guide to Reincarnation, Karma, Astrological Houses, Zodiac Signs, and Moon Phases

© Copyright 2023 — All rights reserved.

The content contained within this book may not be reproduced, duplicated, or transmitted without direct written permission from the author or the publisher.

Under no circumstances will any blame or legal responsibility be held against the publisher, or author, for any damages, reparation, or monetary loss due to the information contained within this book, either directly or indirectly.

Legal Notice:

This book is copyright protected. It is only for personal use. You cannot amend, distribute, sell, use, quote or paraphrase any part, or the content within this book, without the consent of the author or publisher.

Disclaimer Notice:

Please note the information contained within this document is for educational and entertainment purposes only. All effort has been executed to present accurate, up to date, reliable, complete information. No warranties of any kind are declared or implied. Readers acknowledge that the author is not engaging in the rendering of legal, financial, medical, or professional advice. The content within this book has been derived from various sources. Please consult a licensed professional before attempting any techniques outlined in this book.

By reading this document, the reader agrees that under no circumstances is the author responsible for any losses, direct or indirect, that are incurred as a result of the use of information contained within this document, including, but not limited to, errors, omissions, or inaccuracies.

Your Free Gift
(only available for a limited time)

Thanks for getting this book! If you want to learn more about various spirituality topics, then join Mari Silva's community and get a free guided meditation MP3 for awakening your third eye. This guided meditation mp3 is designed to open and strengthen ones third eye so you can experience a higher state of consciousness. Simply visit the link below the image to get started.

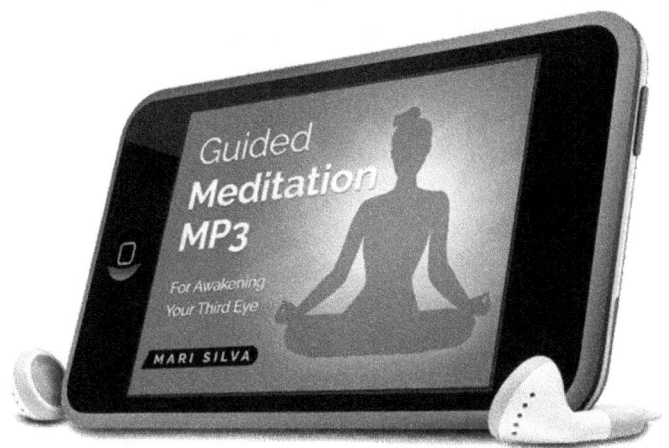

https://spiritualityspot.com/meditation

Table of Contents

INTRODUCTION 1
CHAPTER 1: KARMIC ASTROLOGY 101..3
CHAPTER 2: READING YOUR BIRTH CHART..13
CHAPTER 3: ZODIAC SIGNS AND ELEMENTS..35
CHAPTER 4: PLANETS AND RETROGRADES..45
CHAPTER 5: MOON PHASES AND NODES 54
CHAPTER 6: ASTROLOGICAL HOUSES..66
CHAPTER 7: ALIGN WITH YOUR KARMIC LIFE PURPOSE 75
CHAPTER 8: UNDERSTANDING AND INTEGRATING KARMIC LESSONS 83
CHAPTER 9: ASTROLOGICAL PREDICTIONS...91
CHAPTER 10: REINCARNATION – THE LAW OF KARMIC RETURN........98
CONCLUSION 107
HERE'S ANOTHER BOOK BY MARI SILVA THAT YOU MIGHT LIKE 109
YOUR FREE GIFT (ONLY AVAILABLE FOR A LIMITED TIME) 110
BIBLIOGRAPHY...111

Introduction

If you look at any living being, you will notice certain patterns that all living things have. There is something common between different species and even within specific versions of each specie. The world and even the universe are made up of repetitive patterns, systems, processes, and structures. Karmic astrology is the study of the universe concerning you and how universal forces influence you. More importantly, there is a yin and yang to everything, and every action has an equal and opposite reaction, and there exists a duality in the universe. Through Karmic astrology, you will uncover things about yourself and the world around you that you may not have understood or acknowledged.

However, when discussing something as complex as human existence, its past, or even the future, it cannot be comprehended by a simple explanation. It is presented concisely and simply to the recipient, but much work must be done in the background to make understanding possible. Like how an aircraft looks quite simple when you see it, but you do not see the incredibly complex engineering that happens in the background to make this product a reality.

Similarly, karmic astrology is an interesting way of unraveling secrets about your life; however, it is not as simple as you think. Throughout this book, we will look at all the most important aspects of karmic astrology, what they mean, and how to use them to your advantage. With the knowledge shared in this book, you will evaluate your natal chart and apply this knowledge to any situation because you have the appropriate information at hand.

No part of understanding karmic astrology is more or less important than the other. Everything is important, from the birth chart reading to understanding the moon phases and astrological houses to making karmic predictions. How you apply this information to your life is what makes the difference. While you may only be interested in learning about yourself, you must see things in the bigger picture to really understand things. All nature is intertwined through the universe's fabric, so understanding any one part requires understanding the whole.

Through the information shared in this book, you will learn how to look at the bigger picture and find yourself in this sea of knowledge. Karmic astrology takes time to master, and there is a lot of room for error. The deeper your understanding is, the more you practice, and the more accurately you decipher any situation. Karmic astrology has a history spanning more than two thousand years. Over time, this science has evolved, improved, and expanded. The knowledge of karmic astrology we have at our disposal today is extremely dense and concise, so be ready to spend some time getting your head around it all.

This book is structured specifically to help people with a basic knowledge of karmic astrology or without previous knowledge. Therefore, it will benefit you immensely to go through this book chronologically. Everything is interconnected, and the book has been laid out to make it easier to understand these concepts. Also, keep in mind that these are all predictions and forecasts. Don't be surprised if real-world results vary.

Chapter 1: Karmic Astrology 101

"There is not one Astrology with a capital A. In each epoch, the astrology of the time was a reflection of the kind of order each culture saw in celestial motions, or the kind of relationship the culture formulated between heaven and earth." - Alexander Ruperti

Most people have heard of astrology. However, they often do not realize there are several branches of this discipline. Astrological traditions differ based on the part of the world you live in and what you hope to get from a session with an astrologer.

For example, people new to astrology commonly start a session with someone versed in psychological (also known as modern) astrology or who practices "traditional Western" (Hellenistic, Medieval, etc.) astrology. However, for a different perspective, you can also explore evolutionary astrology, which gives you an understanding of your current and past lives, or Vedic astrology, which is meant for people looking to incorporate astrological suggestions into their daily lives.

Astrologers often consult locational, electional, relationship, and horary astrology specialists when making key life decisions. Of course, these are only a few options available. Another popular alternative is karmic astrology.

What Is Karmic Astrology?

To properly understand what karmic astrology represents, you must first understand the meaning of the two words constituting this discipline: "Karma" and "astrology."

Karma is a concept found in many religions worldwide, and there are almost too many to name. There are many translations of the word; however, you can think about karma as your actions and the result of those actions.

Theological belief holds that a person's karma is a combination of two things: The action a person undertakes and the person who performs that action's intent. This also applies to an action that is planned but never performed—it can affect a person's overall karma as much as a successfully carried-out action can.

You create positive karma when your intentions are good or your actions are positive. If your intentions or actions are bad, your karma is negatively affected. It means that a person can do something positive, but they will still suffer bad karma if their intentions are bad. At the same time, if your intentions are positive, but your actions turn out negative, you can still create good karma for yourself.

In some schools of Hindu theology, a person's karma is inherently linked to the idea of rebirth. Therefore, a person with positive karma will have a better life at rebirth than someone with negative karma. In some schools of thought, a person who dies with negative karma will be reborn as a non-human animal, and the worse your karma, the less significant the animal you are reborn as. However, if you die with positive karma, you will be reborn as a human—the better your karma, the better your position in your next life.

In other schools of thought, having positive karma is one of the requirements for reaching emancipation or moksha—being liberated from the cycle of death and rebirth, and reaching true enlightenment instead. Additionally, Buddhism and Jainism have schools of thought that look at karma differently.

However, most schools of thought in Hinduism, Buddhism, and Jainism feature the theme of causality, essentially indicating a system of cause and effect. If an action happens, it will result in a specific, predetermined reaction.

In the case of karma, it means that a person's actions affect the lives they live, as do the intentions behind them. Specifically, karma holds that deeds, or actions, have like effects, so earning good karma will result in good effects for a person, while earning bad karma will result in bad effects.

It is not always specified what these effects will be, and they may not happen immediately. The effects of karma could appear later in a person's life or future lives. However, it's essential to note that karma is not a system of reward and punishment. Rather, it is a law resulting in consequences.

Astrology concerns how planetary bodies, such as the stars, planets, Sun, and Moon, impact human lives. This practice dates back to at least the second millennium BC and was practiced in several ancient cultures, including the Maya, Hindus, Chinese, Mesopotamians, ancient Greeks, ancient Romans, and Arabs.

As mentioned above, there are several variations of astrology, depending on which geographical tradition you follow and what you hope to learn from a session with an astrologer. In general, there are three major branches:

- **Natal Astrology:** This is the branch most people think of when they hear the word astrology. It makes predictions and analyses based on a person's birth date and time. It often involves charting the sky patterns at the exact moment of your birth (known as a natal chart) and making predictions based on this information. It can also be seen in the popular practice of zodiac-based horoscopes since these predictions are predicated on your date of birth.

- **Mundane Astrology:** This branch of astrology seeks to make predictions about larger matters beyond just a single person. For example, when making predictions about the economy, wars, and other national matters.

- **Interrogatory Astrology:** Like natal astrology, this branch generally focuses on a single person. However, natal astrology makes predictions about the course of a person's life. Interrogatory astrology is more specific, making predictions about specific issues. For example, when is the best date for a person to move home or understand the astrological basis for a specific illness or ailment?

Karmic astrology is most commonly aligned with natal astrology, sharing some similarities. One term commonly used in natal and karmic astrology is houses.

Houses is the term used when referring to a person's natal chart. Once the natal chart is made, it is divided into twelve sections. These sections are known as houses, and a different zodiac sign rules each house. Each house is also linked to a different area of your life, such as relationships, career, communication, etc.

What sign rules what house depends on your time, date, and location of birth, and the way a sign interacts with a certain house affects the analysis of your natal chart.

Understanding Karmic Astrology

Now that you understand what karma and astrology are, it is time to consider the practice of karmic astrology.

As mentioned above, karma involves believing that your actions have positive and negative effects. These effects are not seen instantaneously; some may not even be in your current lifetime but instead reveal themselves in future lives.

That is where karmic astrology comes in.

Like karma, karmic astrology believes that the circumstances of your current life result from past actions of your current life and the effects of unresolved actions in a past life. Karmic astrology offers you the chance to understand the effect of these past lives.

This branch of astrology believes that everything you do and everything that happens to you has a reason rooted in karma. Suppose you want to break your current cycle of mistakes and move forward. In that case, you must understand the karma currently affecting your life. Karmic astrology can help.

For this reason, karmic astrology is occasionally known as past life astrology. It is concerned with helping people identify the problems that have their roots in karma from a past life so they can move forward. Once you understand your current karma, you can take actions to address the issue and fix your karma if you need to.

What Does Karmic Astrology Involve?

You will learn the intricacies of karmic astrology in-depth throughout this book. However, to get you started, here is a basic understanding of what karmic astrology focuses on.

As previously mentioned, your natal chart is divided into twelve sections or houses. A karmic astrology session begins with the creation of your natal chart.

Once your astrologer has created your natal chart, the analysis starts. Karmic astrology focuses on three of the twelve houses: The 4th, 8th, and 12th—all of which are associated with the water element.

- **The Fourth House:** This is the house of your family karma. Just as your karma affects your life, so does your family's karma. This house describes the familial karma you are born under, allowing you to understand what familial habits or patterns you should alter to change your karma.
- **The Eighth House:** This is the house of your partnership karma. It represents karma from your relationships with people beyond your family. The interpretation of this house will help you understand repressed emotional issues and relationship patterns you should take a closer look at and maybe reconsider.
- **The Twelfth House:** This is the house of unredeemed and collective karma. It helps you understand the impact of subconscious service, including actions that you did not take intentionally.

The analysis of your natal chart will also look at the position of the following planetary bodies:

- **Sun:** Helps you understand your life's purpose according to your karma, including your fears, weaknesses, etc.
- **Moon:** Symbolizes a person's karmic past and unresolved issues you carry with you from your past lives mirrored in your current life. The placement of the house of the moon can show negativity in a previous life—where you failed to be as good and true as you could have been. This resulted in an unbalanced experience in that lifetime and is a concern that you will need to resolve through karmic astrology in this lifetime.
- **Saturn:** Other forms of astrology see Saturn as a negative sign and symbol of impending trouble. In karmic astrology, it serves as the judge of your karma. It symbolizes the karmic stumbling blocks you will encounter and will help you move past them. Saturn is so important in karmic astrology that it is sometimes referred to as the "lord of karma."

The two other planetary-bodied karmic astrology focuses on are Rahu and Ketu. These are bodies unique to Hindu texts. Rahu is a shadow entity, considered the entity that causes eclipses and rules meteors. Ketu is considered to be a shadow planet.

In Western astrology, they are known as the north and south lunar nodes. These points show the orbit of the Moon and Earth around the Sun.

- **Rahu/North node:** Rahu represents your karmic path and helps identify your karmic goal or life mission. This goal represents new beginnings and is one that you cannot rely on in your past lives and experiences.
- **Ketu/South node:** Ketu represents your karmic roots and ancestry. It is, essentially, an Achilles heel and serves as a symbol of past issues and karma you want to resolve through your karmic astrology session. It may not necessarily be negative (karma is not necessarily negative), but it is something you need to overcome to move forward and focus on living your present life.

Karmic Astrology, Karmic Debt, and Karmic Relationships

A detailed karmic astrology reading can help you in many ways. One of the primary reasons people seek out these readings is to understand their karmic debt.

Karmic debt is essentially debt you accrued in your past life. It is negative karma you created in a previous life, which you still have to experience. It is something you still have to pay off or debt from a past life.

It's essential to note that karmic debt does not mean a major catastrophe. You can address this debt in various ways and move forward. Once your astrologer has identified any karmic debt you may have, they will also help you move past it.

Another issue many people have in mind when visiting a karmic astrologer is karmic relationships.

Karmic relationships involve two partners in a relationship and their respective karmas. As you now understand, each partner brings their own karma into a relationship and is linked through their karma. From this, we can deduce that those involved previously must use current relationships to learn who they are and how they must act.

A reading focusing on a karmic relationship involves resolving the karmic problem tying the two people together by removing negative karma from one or both partners. These relationships usually fizzle out once the karma linking the two halves is resolved.

It's important to note that the people in a karmic relationship need not be romantically involved. It can be any relationship, including a friend, coworker, parent, or even a pet.

How Good Is Your Karma?

So, you are interested in exploring karmic astrology further, but you're unsure where your karma stands at the moment. If you're wondering how good your karma is, this quiz is for you.

Simply answer each question truthfully, and tally your results based on the instructions at the end of the quiz.

1. You find a wallet abandoned on the train. You decide to:
- a) Find the owner.
- b) Leave it where it is—someone will come and get it soon.
- c) Take out some money and return the wallet.
- d) Keep it for yourself.

2. Do you talk to homeless people?
- a) I would if I needed to.
- b) Perhaps a "hi" as I walk past.
- c) I'd feel a bit nervous doing so.
- d) Never.

3. You do someone a favor. Do you:
- a) Let it stay a secret—you're doing it for them, not for the acknowledgment.
- b) Let them know, but downplay your efforts—you'd like a little acknowledgment but aren't interested in being the center of attention.

- c) Ensure you let the person you helped know—after all, you did it, so they should be aware that you liked them.
- d) Make sure the person you helped knows—you want to ensure they know to pay you back in the future.

4. You encounter a lost and confused tourist on the street. You:
- a) Walk with them to their destination.
- b) Offer to help with directions.
- c) Ignore them and power walk past.
- d) Point and laugh at their predicament with your friends.

5. Do you return books from the library on time?
- a) I return them early more often than not.
- b) I generally return them on time, but I have been late on occasion.
- c) I try returning them on time, but it's hard, and I'm generally late.
- d) I can't remember the last time I returned a library book after checking it out.

6. Do you volunteer?
- a) As much as I can.
- b) Occasionally, but I don't have much time to spare.
- c) I've considered it but have decided against it.
- d) Never—I have limited time and need to focus on making money.

7. Do you recycle?
- a) Always.
- b) As much as possible—although I do slack off occasionally.
- c) When it's convenient.
- d) Never.

8. Your best friend is going through a significant breakup. Do you:
   a) Hang out with them, be there for them, and listen to them for as long as possible.
   b) Spend some time with them and take them out for a meal or two.
   c) Take them out a couple of times.
   d) Offer to split a round of drinks.

9. Would you agree to work at a company whose mission you morally disagreed with in return for a significant salary?
   a) No.
   b) I would consider it, but I'd need a lot more information.
   c) I'd donate some of my paychecks, but yes.
   d) Yes.

10. Do you think people should judge others based on a single action?
    a) No.
    b) Depends on the action in question.
    c) I think judging others on their actions is justified.
    d) Yes—an illegal act should always be given the full book, regardless of personal situations.

Once you have done the quiz, tally your responses. Count how many of each option you got—how many a's, b's, and so on. Determine which choice has the highest number.

Those with the highest number of a's have the best karma, while those with tons of d's need to do a little work to increase their positive karma. Those with more b's and c's have a mix of good and bad karma. If you have more b's, you lean toward positive karma, while those with more c's lean toward negative karma.

Now that you know your karma, the next step is to precisely understand how this affects your karmic astrology reading. The next chapters will cover this, helping you understand how to read your birth chart, explore the importance of zodiac signs and elements, and explain planets, retrogrades, moon phases, and nodes. The chapters will also help you align your life with your karmic life purpose and more.

If you've been curious about your karma and its role in your past and future, you are in the right place. This book about karmic astrology will ensure you know everything important there is to know about this branch of astrology to focus on using it to improve your life and the lives of those around you. All you need to do is turn the page and keep reading as the next chapter helps you to understand how to read your birth chart and explains why it is important.

Chapter 2: Reading Your Birth Chart

You have probably heard of horoscopes more than once in your life. For years, people have used astrological patterns to predict various characteristics of a person. These include personality, mood, luck, fortune, future, and many others. Birth charts are also commonly known as natal charts or, in simpler terms, horoscopes. These charts help you gain tremendous insight into your inner self and psyche.

Birth chart.
https://pxhere.com/en/photo/682841

Understanding Your Birth Chart

A birth chart is a map of where planets are at the moment of a person's birth, situation, relationship, or journey. Specifically, a person's birth chart predicts their individual personality and the key events of their life. A birth chart utilizes constellations and planetary positions to establish an insightful astrological blueprint and provides a roadmap to making good life decisions. Birth charts help reveal the following characteristics of your life:

- Behavioral patterns, healthy and toxic
- Your strengths and weak points
- Relationship compatibility
- Karmic lessons

To read your specific birth chart, you need to know your birth date, time, and place. It is preferable to get the exact time. However, since this information is not always available, use a rough estimate to read your birth chart. The usual layout of a Western birth chart consists of three wheels or circles equally divided into twelve sections, equating to the twelve houses. These three wheels consist of three main components that must be observed. These include the twelve houses, ten planets residing in the twelve houses, and the twelve zodiac signs. Below is what a generic birth chart looks like:

The Inner Wheel

The inner circle represents the location or exact coordinates of your birthplace. It is scientifically proven that the Earth revolves around the Sun instead of the opposite way around. However, astrology focuses on the solar system's interaction with Earth. We can see that the Sun moves around our planet and passes through each sign for around thirty days.

The Mid Wheel

The mid-wheel consists of twelve sections representing the twelve astrological houses. Each section presides over a specific area of your life, including relationships, careers, wealth, luck, etc. The houses start from the ascendant, located in the middle left of your circle, and will move counterclockwise. It is also important to note the position of the ascendant to identify the twelve houses.

Observe a horizontal line that goes through the inner circle to the outer circle. To the left will be your ascendant, or the rising sun representing your worldly personality. This is the personality you use to interact with the rest of the world, and it determines things like your style, looks, temperament, self-esteem, etc. Located to the right is the descendant representing your personality in various relationships, romantic or otherwise.

Next, observe the vertical line, or meridian, which cuts through the middle of the horizontal line. At the bottom, the meridian is the Imum Coeli representing the inner persona of an individual. This part helps identify the person's emotional roots, soul memories, and how they behave privately. Finally, the Midheaven or Medium Coeli is located at the top of the meridian. It embodies your public persona, helping you identify your career path and ambitions and how you can fulfill them to reach your true potential.

The Twelve Sections

The twelve sections consist of the twelve houses, as explained before. These planets exist within different houses, which offers valuable insight into your personality and how you interact with the world. These houses provide a roadmap to understanding your past, present, and future. As the planets move within these regions, different events and changes (physical and mental) occur.

To interpret your birth chart, you first need to observe the locations of the planets in each house. Interestingly, a house can have multiple planets while other houses are empty. So, do not get confused, as it is perfectly normal for the planets and stars to cluster together at the time of someone's birth. The empty houses do not mean there is any deficiency. However, the presence of multiple planets in a house calls for extensive interpretation.

You need to understand the functions of each planet and house to do this and then connect them with the zodiac signs for a complete picture.

The Outer Wheel

As an important concept that arranges the twelve signs of the zodiac—all of which are named after groups of stars—the outer wheel consists of the zodiac signs named after star constellations. Each sign consists of an individual quality or personality. These traits are what distinguish the zodiac signs from one another. These signs will coincide with different houses and create the final interpretation of your birth chart. Here is a simple list of the zodiac signs and their personality traits.

Zodiac Sign	Ruling Planet	Dates	Glyph	Traits
Aries	Mars	20 March - 19 April	♈	Pioneer, Warrior, Daring
Taurus	Venus	20 April - 20 May	♉	Builder, Manifestor
Gemini	Mercury	21 May - 21 June	♊	Networker, Communicator
Cancer	Moon	22 June - 22 July	♋	Nurturer, Motherly
Leo	Sun	23 July - 22 Aug	♌	Performer, Leader
Virgo	Mercury	23 Aug - 22 Sept	♍	Healer, Server, Humble
Libra	Venus	23 Sept - 23 Oct	♎	Diplomat, Delegator
Scorpio	Pluto, Mars	24 Oct - 21 Nov	♏	Psychologist, Transformer
Sagittarius	Jupiter	22 Nov - 21 Dec	♐	Explorer, Philosopher
Capricorn	Saturn	22 Dec - 19 Jan	♑	Timely, Purposeful
Aquarius	Uranus, Saturn	20 Jan - 18 Feb	♒	Reformer, Humanitarian
Pisces	Neptune, Jupiter	19 Feb - 20 March	♓	Dreamer, Compassionate

The Planets

We focus on a total of ten planets when reading the birth chart. Each is located in different houses, depending on your date and place of birth. The energy of these planets influences our lives significantly. However, truly what we do with these energies ultimately decides our fate. Among these planets are the two luminaries, the Sun, and the Moon. Then, we have Mars, Venus, Jupiter, Saturn, Mercury, Uranus, Neptune, and Pluto. These planets are classified into:

Planet	Glyph	Zodiac Sign	House	Description
Sun	☉	Leo	5th	Unique identity, creative potential
Moon	☽	Cancer	4th	Emotions, nurturing feelings
Mercury	☿	Gemini, Virgo	3rd and 6th	Communication, rational thoughts
Mars	♂	Aries, Scorpio	1st and 8th	Motivation, energetic, sexuality
Venus	♀	Taurus, Libra	2nd and 7th	Beauty and art, love, and relationships
Jupiter	♃	Sagittarius, Pisces	9th and 12th	Philosophical, search for answers
Saturn	♄	Capricorn, Aquarius	10th and 11th	Karmic lessons, time restrictions
Uranus	♅	Aquarius	11th	Rebellious, revolutionary feelings
Neptune	♆	Pisces	12th	Change, spiritual awakening
Pluto	♇	Scorpio	8th	Transformation, regeneration, destruction

The Twelve Houses

The twelve houses each represent an aspect of your life and need to be understood in detail. We will delve deeper into the twelve houses in the upcoming chapters. For now, you can get the gist of what each house stands for from this table.

House	Governs	Characteristics
1st House	Self	Appearance, Outward Personality
2nd House	Possessions	Money, Possessions, Values, Skills
3rd House	Communication	Mental Thought Process, Communication, Siblings
4rth House	Family and Home	Home, Parents, Roots, Inner Security
5th House	Pleasure	Romance, Children, Creativity, Fun
6th House	Health	Work, Health, Self-Improvement
7th House	Partnerships	Marriage and Other Relationships
8th House	Sex	Sex, Death, Regeneration, Sharing
9th House	Philosophy	Higher Education, Philosophy, Religion, Travel, Law
10th House	Social Status	Career, Status, Reputation, Vocational Purpose

11th House	Friendships	Friends, Groups, Goals, Aspirations
12th House	Subconscious	Solitude, Transcendance, Institutions, Self-Sabotage

How to Interpret Your Birth Chart

Once you have learned about the various zodiac signs, planets, and houses, it is time to interpret your birth chart First, generate your birth chart using an online source, or draw it up if you are an expert. Next, consider the zodiac sign and house each planet is in. Do not try to read all the planets at once. First, narrow down on a single planet and identify the house it is present in and its associated zodiac sign. Once you've done this, list and interpret them according to the following functions:

Planets — Represent what drives you, what you enjoy

Houses — Represent where you should expect growth or change

Zodiacs — Represent the manner of accomplishing a task

For instance, let us assume your birth chart has Uranus in Aries, in the fourth house. List that down and refer back to the tables and data you've learned above. From that, we can conclude:

Planet — Uranus (Ability to learn, grow, revolutionize)

House — Fourth House (Home and family)

Zodiac — Aries (passionate, ambitious, strong)

From this information, we can interpret that you're very passionate about your family and home, and you learn and grow mostly through your loved ones. Your emotional well-being is mainly connected with your roots, so your happiness depends on your family.

Exercise: Try Interpreting;

Here is an example birth chart to try your hand at interpreting the different meanings and insights.

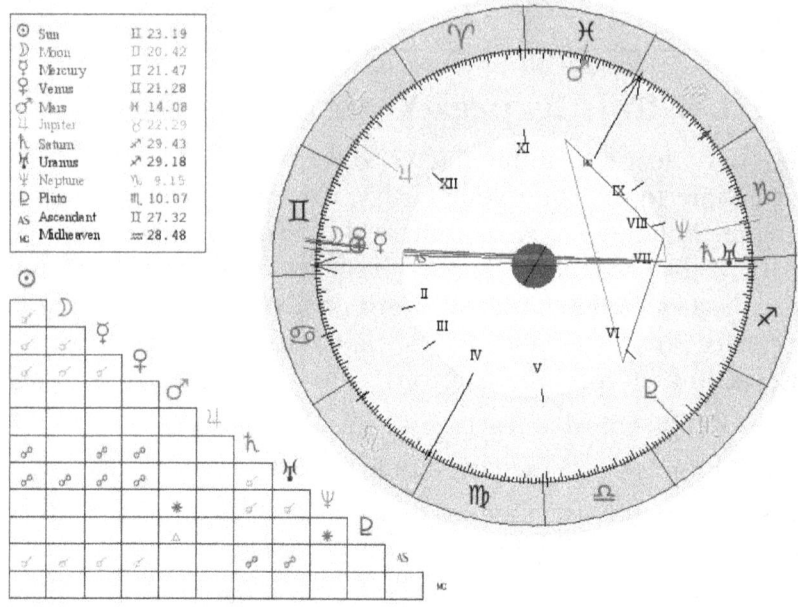

Birth chart and their interpretations.
https://commons.wikimedia.org/wiki/File:Birth_chart_example.JPG

1st House

    Planet _____

    House _____

    Zodiac _____

    Interpretation

_____

_____

_____

_____

    Planet _____

    House _____

    Zodiac _____

Interpretation
_____
_____
_____
_____

2nd House
Planet _____
House _____
Zodiac _____
Interpretation
_____
_____
_____
_____

4th House
Planet _____
House _____
Zodiac _____
Interpretation
_____
_____
_____
_____

Planet _____
House _____
Zodiac _____
Interpretation
_____
_____
_____
_____

8th House
Planet _____
House _____
Zodiac _____

Interpretation
_____
_____
_____

Planet _____
House _____
Zodiac _____
Interpretation
_____
_____
_____

9th House
   Planet _____
   House _____
   Zodiac _____
   Interpretation
_____
_____
_____

10th House
   Planet _____
   House _____
   Zodiac _____
   Interpretation
_____
_____
_____

11th House
   Planet _____
   House _____
   Zodiac _____

Interpretation

_____
_____
_____
_____

12th House
  Planet _____
  House _____
  Zodiac _____
  Interpretation

_____
_____
_____
_____

For You: Worksheets

Now, generate birth charts and use the following worksheets to interpret your birth chart or your friends' and loved ones' charts.

1st House
  Planet _____
  House _____
  Zodiac _____
  Interpretation

_____
_____
_____

  Planet _____
  House _____
  Zodiac _____
  Interpretation

_____
_____
_____
_____

2nd House

Planet _____

House _____

Zodiac _____

Interpretation

_____

_____

_____

_____

Planet _____

House _____

Zodiac _____

Interpretation

_____

_____

_____

_____

3rd House

Planet _____

House _____

Zodiac _____

Interpretation

_____

_____

_____

_____

Planet _____

House _____

Zodiac _____

Interpretation

_____

_____

_____

_____

4th House

    Planet _____

    House _____

    Zodiac _____

    Interpretation

    _____
    _____
    _____
    _____

    Planet _____

    House _____

    Zodiac _____

    Interpretation

    _____
    _____
    _____
    _____

5th House

    Planet _____

    House _____

    Zodiac _____

    Interpretation

    _____
    _____
    _____
    _____

    Planet _____

    House _____

    Zodiac _____

    Interpretation

    _____
    _____
    _____
    _____

6th House

Planet _____

House _____

Zodiac _____

Interpretation

_____

_____

_____

_____

Planet _____

House _____

Zodiac _____

Interpretation

_____

_____

_____

_____

7th House

Planet _____

House _____

Zodiac _____

Interpretation

_____

_____

_____

_____

Planet _____

House _____

Zodiac _____

Interpretation

_____

_____

_____

_____

8th House

Planet _____
House _____
Zodiac _____
Interpretation
_____
_____
_____
_____

Planet _____
House _____
Zodiac _____
Interpretation
_____
_____
_____
_____

9th House

Planet _____
House _____
Zodiac _____
Interpretation
_____
_____
_____
_____

Planet _____
House _____
Zodiac _____
Interpretation
_____
_____
_____
_____

10th House

Planet _____

House _____

Zodiac _____

Interpretation

_____
_____
_____
_____

Planet _____

House _____

Zodiac _____

Interpretation

_____
_____
_____
_____

11th House

Planet _____

House _____

Zodiac _____

Interpretation

_____
_____
_____
_____

Planet _____

House _____

Zodiac _____

Interpretation

_____
_____
_____
_____

12th House
    Planet _____
    House _____
    Zodiac _____
    Interpretation
    _____
    _____
    _____
    _____

    Planet _____
    House _____
    Zodiac _____
    Interpretation
    _____
    _____
    _____
    _____

KEY

(For interpretation of the first and last planet in the exercise birth chart)

Rising Sign (28 Degrees Sagittarius)

Even though you can be infamous for your indiscretion and bluntness, you are actually quite open, honest, and outgoing. No one should take anything you say personally because you mean no harm. Living your life in a straightforward manner is highly appreciated, but you consider social niceties an obstacle to true communication. You possess lots of energy and will become restless if restricted. You enjoy freedom as opposed to being anxious and feeling trapped. You enjoy the outdoors, where you can express your freedom and energy, and so you enjoy sports and socializing, and you will liven up any gathering.

Planet 1 — Mars (ambitious, courageous, energetic)

House — First House (self-esteem, unique identity)

Zodiac — Capricorn (purposeful, timely)

Interpretation: Extremely ambitious, you are willing to work very hard to reach your goals. You're very practical, cautious, and conservative. You require concrete results for all your effort, and you manage to excel in whatever you set your mind to. You own a great sense of responsibility and self-discipline. However, make sure not to judge others.

Planet 11 — Pluto (transformation, rebirth, regeneration)

House — Twelfth House (subconscious, transcendence)

Zodiac — Sagittarius (explorer, philosopher)

Interpretation: Society's cherished beliefs and totems will be radically changed for your entire generation. Many traditional concepts will be entirely altered, if not destroyed completely. The rights of individuals to pursue their own course in life will be reasserted.

Rising Sign (Sagittarius)

This is a person with an open personality, known for their frankness and honesty. However, they can be, at times, blunt and insensitive, which usually offends people. People close to this person have learned not to take everything they say personally because of their indiscreet nature. This person appreciates the simplicities in life and considers social formalities and niceties barriers to real and effective communication. Therefore, this person would rather be straightforward and simple than opt for a formal approach to a conversation.

This person has lots of pent-up energy and, if not dissipated in some way, can become restless and feel confined. Furthermore, this person loves the outdoors and demands freedom, whether freedom of speech or to do as they like. Their lack of conforming to social niceties does not make them any less of a social person; their lively spirit and enthusiasm make them very popular in social gatherings.

First House

Planet — Mars (ambitious, courageous, energetic)

House — First House (self-esteem, unique identity)

Zodiac — Capricorn (purposeful, timely)

Interpretation: The ruling planet is Mars, and this person is extremely ambitious about their goals and aims. They will do anything necessary to achieve their set goals. The zodiac Capricorn adds a trait of purposefulness to their personality. This person is very practical about their goals and demands tangible results within time limits. Their unique identity is very responsible, they are dedicated to their goals, and have a keen sense of self-discipline that lets them succeed in their tasks. However, this person tends to judge others by their status and prestige and always looks at others as competition.

Planet — Neptune (change-loving, spiritually awakened)
House — First House (self-esteem, unique identity)
Zodiac — Aquarius (reformer, humanitarian)

Interpretation: As a reformer, who loves to bring change, this person will idealize the ability to analyze any given situation objectively. They will work on many humanitarian causes to cure society of its many flaws and injustices taking place every day. However, they will have to be very careful when working toward change and for the rights of individuals amid a fast-changing society.

Second House

Planet — Uranus (rebellious, revolutionary)
House — Second House (money, possessions, values, skills)
Zodiac — Aquarius (reformer, humanitarian)

Interpretation: A reformer at heart, this person likes to bring about positive changes all around them. Whether it is for their friends, peers, or society in general, positive change drives this person. They are willing to devote their time, effort, money, skills, and energy to a purpose. However, due to their humanitarian personality, they can often end up neglecting their personal relationships.

Fourth House

Planet — Jupiter (philosophical, in search of answers)
House — Fourth House (home, parents, roots)
Zodiac — Aries (pioneer, warrior)

Interpretation: This person is well known for being an uncompromising individualist who grows and develops philosophically and needs to explore their hidden talents and abilities. Focused primarily on their roots and family, they are pioneers and warriors when fighting for their families. They take pride in their accomplishments. However, they can become self-centered and sometimes ignore the needs of the people around them.

Planet — Saturn (karmic lessons, time limitations)
House — Fourth House (home, parents, roots)
Zodiac — Taurus (builder, manifester)

Interpretation: With a builder's personality, this person needs proper order in their life and to feel stable and secure. While they want to see change around them, they are not entirely open to adapting to new and unpredictable situations. They often experience karmic lessons and learn from them every time. However, their constant fear of the unknown makes them seem withdrawn and anxious. So, it's important that they surround themselves with supportive people to become more emotionally stable and self-supporting.

Eighth House

Planet — North node

House — Eighth House (sex, death, regeneration, sharing)

Zodiac — Leo (performer, leader)

Interpretation: Considered a natural leader, this person does not shy away from the opportunity to lead others toward completing their goals. They enjoy organizing and delegating group activities. Due to their enthusiastic and strong personality, others listen when they give suggestions and actually implement them in their work. Unlike most leaders, they are not patronizing or overly domineering in their interactions. This person also has a big, attention-grabbing personality and enjoys being in the spotlight whenever there is a large gathering. People usually love this person as long as they do not become arrogant or self-centered.

Planet — Moon (emotions, nurturing feelings)

House — Eighth House (sex, death, regeneration, sharing)

Zodiac — Virgo (healer, server, humble)

Interpretation: This person is seriously minded and cheerful at the same time. They have a stellar sense of humor, an enthusiastic personality, and a focused mind. They prefer tasks that can help them stay engaged mentally and physically. This person is considered a careful worker and will go out of their way to help others without ever being snobby about it. Their most prominent traits include practicality, reliability, efficiency, and enthusiasm. They are sometimes considered a prude but entirely devoted and caring to those they love.

Ninth House

Planet — Venus (beauty and art, love, and relationships)

House — Ninth House (higher education, philosophy, religion, travel, law)

Zodiac — Virgo (healer, server, humble)

Interpretation: This person expresses their love and affection by serving people selflessly. They often doubt their self-worth and have low self-esteem issues in relationships. This should be avoided, and they must learn to love themselves—just as they are—and then pursue other relationships. Their standards of love and perfection are very high, and they are often attracted to people based on a sense of duty or responsibility instead of genuine interest. Furthermore, they can sometimes be superficial about themselves and others, which leads to them alienating anyone they start to get close to.

Tenth House

Planet — Sun (unique identity, creative potential)

House — Tenth House (career, status, reputation, vocational purpose)

Zodiac — Scorpio (psychologist, transformer)

Interpretation: While they prefer a straightforward approach to life, this person is actually very complex and intense by nature. Their emotions in critical situations are very strong. However, they find it very difficult to express their emotions in detail and rather opt for a simplistic approach. This person might be social and popular but needs alone time to recharge and process their emotions in peace. They are usually calm and collected but become completely unforgiving when angered. They have a ton of creative potential and are very serious about their careers. They are known to be willful, tenacious, and passionate about their careers and reputations.

Eleventh House

Planet — Mercury (communication, rational thoughts)

House — Eleventh House (friends, groups, goals, aspirations)

Zodiac — Sagittarius (explorer, philosopher)

Interpretation: They have an explorative, curious, and inquisitive mind and are always looking for rational answers and logical explanations. They are interested in broad subject matters, whether philosophy, science, or religion. Their aspirations lie in abstract details associated with any subject, and they usually focus on small details.

Twelfth House

Planet — Pluto (transformation, regeneration, destruction)

House — Twelfth House (solitude, transcendence, institutions, self-Sabotage)

Zodiac — Sagittarius (explorer, philosopher)

Interpretation: When working toward change and transformation, they will see their efforts successfully regenerating society's cherished beliefs and radically changing fundamental concepts. They will reassert individuals' rights to pursue their own course in life and explore different philosophies.

Chapter 3: Zodiac Signs and Elements

The term zodiac in astronomy or astrology defines a band in the sky that the Sun, Moon, and other planets pass through, as seen from Earth. The zodiac consists of various constellations, and the Sun or other celestial bodies move through these constellations with time. The ancient Greeks and Romans divided these constellations into zodiacs and believed the position of the celestial bodies could predict future events. This gave rise to the concept of astronomical zodiacs and their associated meanings.

The zodiac symbols.
https://pxhere.com/en/photo/1001293

Every individual is assigned a zodiac sign based on the constellation the Sun was in when they were born. Astronomers believe these zodiac signs predict a lot about a person, from their likes and dislikes to their personality and possibly even some aspects of their future. As discussed in the previous chapter, these predictions are made by a birth chart. In addition, it is important to learn about the different zodiac signs and what they convey about a person. This chapter will detail the twelve zodiac signs, what elements they are associated with, and the qualities of each sign.

Zodiac Signs

1. Aries

People with Aries as their zodiac sign are often ambitious, motivated, and headstrong. This fierceness is due to Mars as the governing planet for this zodiac sign. Both witty and humorous, Aries people are good with social networks and persuasive to almost everyone around them. Although they get mad easily, it is also easy to calm them down. They will start any project with full zest and motivation but often find themselves scattered and diverted.

Aries personalities have positive and negative sides. Aries have strong personalities, not easily discouraged by minor setbacks. They have a unique zest for living and show an active and energetic spirit. However, they can be callous and insensitive when communicating in a conflicting situation.

2. Taurus

A dominating feature of this sign is their strength and strong will. The associated planet, Venus, further makes these individuals emotional. Stubborn and unwilling to change, Taurus people are somewhat rigid. However, their empathetic nature makes them worth the trouble. Logic and reasoning will not affect them much, but emotions and feelings more easily persuade them.

Taurus people are opportunists, so they go along with whatever comes their way instead of finding opportunities, which often limits their success. However, when they have money, they are very generous with it, especially with friends and loved ones. The positive side of Taurus is that they are honest and forthright in all their dealings because of their empathic nature. However, they often find it hard to trust people completely and are suspicious of everyone around them.

3. Gemini

In contrast to the previous zodiac, Gemini's key characteristic is adaptability and flexibility. The readiness to change in Geminis is indeed remarkable, which helps them make instantaneous decisions. The governing planet, Mercury, makes this trait in Geminis even stronger, resulting in an act-now-explain-later approach. This approach often comes in handy in tricky situations in the workplace or field. Geminis are imaginative, generous, and humble to those around them.

Their frequent need for change makes it impossible for existing conditions to satisfy them. The positive side of Geminis is observed in their quick wit, open-mindedness, and intellectual nature. Creativity and innovation stem naturally in their minds. However, due to the ever-changing nature of their ideas, they often do multiple things at once and end up getting side-tracked and finishing nothing.

4. Cancer

This sign's ruling planet is the Moon, and just like it, the zodiac is associated with shifting tides and personality changes. These individuals cling to traditions and culture but keep up with changing times. This contradicting nature can be associated with the fluid nature of the Moon. Cancers love to stick with their family and spend time in the comfort of their homes, yet they also love to travel to new places. People with this zodiac are highly sensitive but do not show it to people around them. They hate arguments and would rather avoid conflict than face it. They are also not great at receiving criticism and often take it to heart.

The perk of being highly sensitive is that they are extremely compassionate to the people around them. They cannot bear to see others get hurt, especially because of them. Cancers are often resigned to fate when they can't take hardships anymore. They will hide in their shells and lack the initiative to do things requiring them to go out of their way. This trait especially hinders their road to success.

5. Leo

Leos have powerful, dominating personalities and are considered born leaders. The governing planet is the Sun, which gives Leos the light to shine brilliantly. Leos are ambitious and idealistic, making them susceptible to the failure of their shortcomings. They are high-minded and intellectual. However, they are also often high-handed, resulting in overconfident mistakes.

Their impulsive nature makes them easy targets for small failures in daily tasks, but they are brave enough to stand back up and try again. Their magnetic attitude attracts people, and their charming personalities easily win them over. Leos are optimistic, energetic, and generous. You will never see a Leo being stingy when treating others. However, they can be a bit arrogant about their position and power and often mistreat others. Egocentricity is a common trait among Leos.

6. Virgo

Virgos are analyzers of deep and interesting subjects and are often the most intellectual minds of all the zodiacs. The ruling planet, Mercury, makes their decisions more impulsive, which is often a weakness for their capable minds. Their persuasive skills are among the best, convincing even the most stubborn people. Their inquiring minds don't let them rest until they have all the answers they seek.

They are good at analyzing a situation by extracting information from people and making accurate assumptions about any missing information to create a clear picture. Unlike other zodiacs, Virgos are consistent with their work and always finish their tasks to near perfection. However, this quality also brings out some bad qualities in their personality. They think their work is superior to others and are sometimes too critical of colleagues.

7. Libra

Libras are extra nice and make just decisions regarding their friendships and relationships. They try to keep everything in balance and promote goodwill, peace, and friendships, even if they have to go out of their way to do so. Their ruling planet, Venus, makes them attracted to beauty and art. Their sympathetic nature makes it impossible for them to say no to a friend or family member in need. They would even stick up for a stranger if they thought they were being mistreated.

Their intuition is especially strong, which helps them sniff out any deceit or misinformation others may present. However, in their quest to make everything right and balanced, they are often insincere and lie to prevent any relationship imbalance. It could mean they give in easily in arguments even if they know they are right so as not to escalate the situation any further.

8. Scorpio

Scorpios are fearless individuals, confident in themselves, and guided by their self-control and boldness. Their ruling planet, Mars, only adds to the fuel of the already passionate Scorpios and gives them the will to face any challenges and obstacles that might come their way. Scorpios are secretive, sensitive, and very observant. However, once they're roused to take action, nothing can stand in the way of their success.

When they work for others, they rise very high, but they can often become domineering and aggressive, resulting in their ultimate downfall. It is their greatest weakness. Scorpios are natural fighters if the opportunity presents itself. However, they can act hypersensitive in many situations and boast about themselves to deal with neglect from their loved ones. Another weakness is that they have no hold over their temper and are easily angered.

9. Sagittarius

Sagittarius individuals are hard workers and give their best when working on a project. However, they have trouble concentrating on projects of immediate importance. From their governing planet, Jupiter, they get a happy, cheerful, and vibrant personality that combines with their zest and hard work for the perfect score. However, Sagittarius people often overwork themselves and struggle with anxiety throughout their projects. Therefore, they should focus primarily on rewarding projects that make their struggles worthwhile. Sagittarians are the most friendly and easygoing people of all zodiacs. A great weakness of Sagittarians is their financial mismanagement. They are often attracted to gambling and other vices.

10. Capricorn

This sign produces deep, philosophical thinkers and scholars. Their intellect also helps them apply their knowledge to practical life. When working on a specific thing, they will be deliberate and calm. Unlike many impulsive zodiac signs, Capricorns exhibit a drive and passion for knowledge but approach it in a scholarly fashion. Capricorns tend to be loners and prefer solitude to complete their tasks. However, this trait leaves them feeling lonely sometimes. They are charitable, generous, and humble to people deserving of help. To friends, Capricorns are the most loyal and trustworthy of all zodiacs. Sometimes, they may also act too bossy and drive people away. They can also be excessively critical of others and offend people when working together.

11. Aquarius

Aquarius zodiacs are mostly devoted to humanitarian causes and look toward making life easier for people. They take on great missions to help people and have a friendly attitude, making them comfortable to be friends with. Their governing planet, Saturn, provides them with the energy and willpower needed to complete their tasks with quiet determination. They are loners, too, but unlike Capricorns, Aquarius people do not mind company when they get it.

Aquarius people are very tolerant and considerate, making them quite popular. Yet they still prefer working in solitude to focus on the task at hand completely. Aquarius people are dreamers but can get carried away by their dreams and seem rather eccentric to others. They don't like admitting their faults and mistakes, resulting in fanatic views.

12. Pisces

Pisces people are the most unassuming bunch of the whole zodiac. They are so humble that they fail to give themselves credit even when they're knowledgeable about certain things and let others take the credit. The governing planet, Jupiter, endows these individuals with an extremely generous nature that they let others walk all over them. They fail to snatch opportunities and let others take the spotlight in these circumstances.

The humbler they are, the more they doubt their abilities. This ultimately results in worry and anxiety. Pisces people are the most cautious of all the zodiac and will think multiple times before they take a leap. The philosophical nature of this zodiac often results in individuals being talented in music, art, or other creative activities. However, Pisces people miss out on good opportunities and become depressed and gloomy about life because of their cautious attitude.

Elements

The zodiacs are further understood by two main factors that classify them into certain categories. These include elements and qualities. Elements speak to the fundamental nature of a sign, whereas qualities are concerned with how the signs express themselves. Air, Earth, Fire, and Water were implemented by the ancient Greeks as the building blocks for the universe and everything within it. Each zodiac sign is associated with one of these four elements. These elements describe the basic nature of an individual's persona. To properly understand zodiac signs, we must understand what these elements represent.

1. Earth

Virgo, Taurus, and Capricorn are all earth signs. Anyone linked to these signs is generally a secure and stable person, grounded in reality. They are not much for taking risks and avoiding conflict. The earth element represents building or creating things, so earth zodiacs desire to create or build things in their lives. Whether these are solid, physical, or strong emotional aspects, earth elementals are all about stability.

It can be as simple as creating comfortable rooms in a home or creating jobs or opportunities for others. Zodiacs with the earth element are influenced to accumulate worldly possessions around them for a sense of stability. However, this trait can turn into an unhealthy habit when individuals become greedy or materialistic.

The earth element represents a sense of duty and responsibility, and zodiacs associated with the earth element feel a need to help and support people around them. Earth elementals are logical and take a measured approach that guarantees little to no risk. However, these people are so focused on the outcome that they sometimes overlook other people's feelings. In short, zodiacs supported by earth have their feet on the ground and their eyes on the prize.

2. Air

Libra, Gemini, and Aquarius are all air signs. The zodiacs graced by this element have the added benefit of intellect. These individuals are smart thinkers and can reason abstractly. Their intellect is coupled with their creative mind to bring forth critical thinkers. Air sign zodiacs are all about communicating their thoughts and ideas to the world.

They analyze things deeply and can be pretty useful in a dilemma. Air signs are neither too feisty nor too calm. Depending on their mood, they can have a calm and collected attitude like a fresh breeze but can be easily angered like the howling wind. Air signs are humane and often look toward helping others as much as they can. With their objective thinking and cooperative nature, no issue is too difficult for them to solve.

3. Water

Associated with Cancer, Scorpio, and Pisces, water represents the fluid nature of these zodiacs. Water is fluid, wavering, and flowing, and so are the qualities of these zodiacs. Water zodiacs have a higher sense of intuition and feel everything at a much higher intensity than others. These signs are emotional and nurturing and often act on emotions rather than logic.

Water signs are very compassionate to others, feel their problems as their own, and will seek solutions for them. Those supported by water are all about beautiful and aesthetic things, whether art, music, or nature. They desire beauty and want others to be happy because of this beauty. Much like water, these zodiacs, if stagnant, can lose their way and become self-indulgent.

4. Fire

Sagittarius, Aries, and Leo are all fire signs. As expected, the zodiacs graced by fire are indeed ferocious. These signs are passionate, ambitious, and never lacking in courage. However, just like fire, it becomes very difficult to contain them if they get out of control. The fire element gives these zodiacs lively spirits and a well of creativity. The people graced by the fire element are self-confident, spontaneous, and have a tremendous zest for life. These signs are the most passionate in a love match.

Qualities

The quality of a zodiac defines an individual's attitude to life and how they approach projects and different tasks. The qualities are explained below:

1. Cardinal

Cancer, Aries, Capricorn, and Libra have cardinal qualities. These signs are the initiators of the zodiac, plus they are located at the jumping-off points on the chart wheel of birth charts. Aries is placed at the ascendant, and so on. Signs with a cardinal quality want to get things started. They are ambitious, quick, and active. Cardinals start many projects but fail to complete them successfully because signs with this quality are more interested in starting things than finishing them. Cardinal energy can sometimes seem overbearing, but this drive helps them complete many tasks.

2. Fixed

Fixed qualities are associated with Scorpio, Taurus, Leo, and Aquarius. These individuals prefer steadiness over pace. They will work on their projects calmly and collectedly and get them to completion. These individuals are determined to complete their tasks and have a stable approach to problem-solving. Fixed quality signs are highly self-reliant and never doubt themselves as they move steadily toward their goals. On the flip side, these signs can be rigid and stubborn to changing environments.

3. Mutable

Virgo, Pisces, Gemini, and Sagittarius are mutable signs that are more flexible in their approach to life. These individuals are willing to change their behavior, approach, and expressions depending on the circumstances. They are highly resourceful and well-liked by others because of their flexible personalities. They have a strong sixth sense that helps them scope out possible opportunities and shape them in ways that help the most. However, their desire to please everyone is the same one that gets them into trouble.

Here is an easy-to-understand chart summarizing the learnings and understandings of zodiac signs and their characteristics.

Zodiac Sign	Ruling Planet	Symbol	Glyph	Quality	Element
Aries	Mars	Ram	♈	Cardinal	Fire
Taurus	Venus	Bull	♉	Fixed	Earth
Gemini	Mercury	Twins	♊	Mutable	Air
Cancer	Moon	Crab	♋	Cardinal	Water
Leo	Sun	Lion	♌	Fixed	Fire
Virgo	Mercury	Virgin	♍	Mutable	Earth
Libra	Venus	Scales	♎	Cardinal	Air

Zodiac Sign	Ruling Planet	Symbol	Glyph	Quality	Element
Scorpio	Pluto, Mars	Scorpion	♏	Fixed	Water
Sagittarius	Jupiter	Archer	♐	Mutable	Fire
Capricorn	Saturn	Sea goat	♑	Cardinal	Earth
Aquarius	Uranus, Saturn	Water bearer	♒	Fixed	Air
Pisces	Neptune, Jupiter	Fish	♓	Mutable	Water

The development of zodiacs has a rich history in astronomy. While it started by associating individuals with their birth zodiac sign, modern astrology considers all twelve zodiacs. It combines these with the twelve houses and the position of the planets on each occasion. This combined information gives us a much clearer picture of our horoscope than a simple zodiac prediction. Each zodiac sign is ruled by single or multiple planets that significantly impact their characteristics. Similarly, each of the qualities and elements impacts how a certain zodiac's traits and characteristics are shaped. Thus, each factor has a unique significance when interpreting someone's zodiac signs or natal chart readings.

Chapter 4: Planets and Retrogrades

The Earth is surrounded by two luminary bodies, the Sun, the Moon, and eight planets. Each body carries a profound amount of energy specific to it. These planetary energies affect you on every level.

It is not only their energy that influences your life but also their movements. These bodies revolve around the Sun and cross paths with the twelve zodiac signs of the universe. Every zodiac sign carries its energy, so when a planetary body meets a zodiac sign, it creates a different energy field affecting your life.

This chapter will teach you about the planets' movements and pace. You will also learn how these seemingly subtle movements influence your life in space.

Pace

In astrology, planets are divided into two groups, inner and outer planets. Inner planets move much quicker than outer planets, meaning you feel their effects more than you would feel the movement of outer planets.

As the planets go around the natal chart, they create aspects. Aspects are certain angles created by the planets. These angles are an expression of the energy that two planets create together.

Inner Planets

☉ Sun

This luminary body moves one degree every day in your natal chart. It means it remains in the same zodiac sign for thirty days and takes 360 days to return to the same degree as your natal sun. Due to its fast pace, aspects created by the Sun last for three days.

The Sun represents your core personality and ego. It is important that you understand that it only reflects who you are at heart, but it's not an expression of who you are as a complex being. It represents your masculine side, along with your charisma, confidence, and creativity.

When the Sun moves around, you start questioning your identity. The feelings this movement might inspire in you solely depend on its aspects. Harsh aspects can make you dissatisfied with yourself, while soft aspects create a harmonious environment.

☾ Moon

On average, the Moon travels to the next sign within two to two and a half days. It means that the Moon takes twenty-eight days to complete its cycle around the chart. Its aspects last for three hours.

The Moon is your emotions and represents your feminine side. It includes your intuition, softness, vulnerabilities, and nurturing side.

Your emotions are entirely vulnerable to the movements of the Moon. You will experience emotional fluctuation whenever the Moon travels to a different sign or has aspects with other planets.

☿ Mercury

Mercury spends about three weeks in one sign and completes its cycle after 88 days. Usually, the aspects it creates last for approximately two days.

This planet represents your mind, including communication skills and style, cognitive and intellectual abilities, perception, and thought patterns. It is mostly responsible for the conscious side of your brain and relates more to logic than the abstract. Mercury also represents short travels, affecting things like vehicles and various transportation means.

Depending on the planet's newly found location, you might experience mental fluctuations—experiences on the road or with your car. It can affect your traveling, especially the journey on your way there.

♀ Venus

Venus usually stations for eighteen days in one sign when traveling around the signs and then moves on. It takes 224.5 days to complete its cycle, and its aspects last for two days.

Venus is the planet of relationships, love, life, beauty, and finances. The planet rules all relationships and is not limited to romance. It is also associated with art, possessions, social life, sensuality, and pleasure.

Relationships and other Venusian life aspects might undergo periodic shifts with the planet's movements and aspects. However, even if you are experiencing a harsh aspect, it will only last a few days.

♂ Mars

Mars spends around two months in one sign and twenty-two months to cover the whole natal chart. Its aspects last for approximately a week.

This planet rules physical activities, sexual energy, force, aggression, animalistic behavior, bravery, and desire. It is also connected to weaponry, violence, war, and accidents.

Mars's effects are usually felt because of its strong impact. So, when it moves, you may find yourself in situations that come out of nowhere. They could be forceful and disruptive to your daily routine.

Depending on its placement and aspects, you may find yourself in a fight you did not initiate or become aggravated easily and feel anger surging through your veins without a specific reason.

♃ Jupiter

Jupiter lingers for a whole year under one sign, meaning it completes its journey every twelve years. The aspects it creates usually last for three weeks.

Jupiter is known as the planet of good fortune. It also rules long-distance traveling, philosophy, the abstract mind, philosophy, religion, indulgence, leisure, luck, growth, and prosperity.

There is usually nothing to worry about with this planet's movement because it will bring you good fortune wherever it may be. However, the only factor that could dull your good luck is the difficult aspects of Jupiter.

Outer Planets

♄ Saturn

Saturn spends two and a half years in each sign and takes twenty-nine and a half years to reach its natal placement. The aspects it creates last for six weeks on average.

Known as the teacher, Saturn rules discipline, order, ambition, responsibility, tradition, and patience. It causes limitations and restrictions to teach you about something that you lack.

This planet is somewhat feared because it may take blessings away from your life. However, this only lasts for a short time. You will be immune to its effects once you have learned your lessons.

♅ Uranus

Uranus spends seven years in each sign and takes around 84 years to land in its natal placement. Its aspects last for three months.

This planet is associated with originality, eccentricity, rebelliousness, innovation, technology, magic, psychology, and astrology. It causes sudden changes and disruption. It is concerned with humanitarian issues and is futuristic within itself. Naturally, it affects humanitarian causes and supports innovative and futuristic ideas.

This planet's effects are often unexpected because they depend on what house it is in and its aspects with other planets. So, check your transit Uranus to know what changes you might experience during the seven years.

♆ Neptune

Neptune stays fourteen years in each sign and takes 164 to complete a full cycle around the natal chart. Its aspects last for two years on average.

This planet rules the water bodies, art, music, spirituality, illusions, dreams, subconscious, drugs, drug abuse, hypnosis, sleepwalking, and trances.

Generally, Neptune's effects are not immediately felt. It will take some time to settle into a sign, and then it creates certain themes in your life for fourteen years. You can learn about your Neptunian effects by studying the sign it is currently in.

♇ Pluto

Pluto stays in each sign anywhere from fourteen to thirty years. It might take around 248 years to complete its cycle around your birth chart. Its aspects may last several weeks, but it depends on its speed in your chart.

Pluto is an intense planet. It rules anything hidden, death, rebirth, transformation, obsessions, phobias, beginnings, endings, and isolation. It also rules dark things like coercion, kidnappings, viruses, and bacteria.

Typically, Pluto is perceived as the planet of transformation. So, wherever it is in your natal chart, it transforms you based on its current placement. You must study its current sign and compare it to your natal Pluto to interpret this planet's effects correctly.

Planets in Retrograde

Now that you have an idea about the planets' movements, it is time to learn about planetary retrogrades. Retrograde is a planetary movement where the planets appear to be moving backward for a certain period and then return to their normal pattern.

The planets do not move backward. The Earth just moves faster than the planet's orbit. So, the planet seems like it is moving backward.

Mercury

Mercury retrograde. Even if you are unfamiliar with astrology, you have probably heard of this term somewhere. This phenomenon happens approximately three times a year and usually lasts three weeks.

There are a few advantages and disadvantages to this periodic movement. During this time, you might feel nostalgic. You may be thinking about your favorite things from childhood or entertaining your nostalgia and experiencing fond moments.

Another advantage is reconnecting with people. This planet rules communication, so it makes sense that when it is in retrograde, you reconnect with the friends you have lost touch with.

One of the disadvantages you could deal with during this time is technology and transportation issues. It's also rather easy to create conflict during this period because there is much room for communication.

You should be mindful of your communication and ensure you understand people correctly to avoid misunderstandings.

Astrologists warn against signing contracts because your cognitive abilities are usually slightly clouded.

Venus

Venus goes into retrograde approximately every eighteen months and lasts about forty days. This planet is closest to Earth, so its effects are significantly powerful. Its retrograde digs up repressed relationship issues and brings them to the surface.

Discussing relationship issues could be considered a disadvantage, but Venus wants you to heal and experience healthier relationships, so it helps you by bringing them up.

You could also come face-to-face with your physical insecurities, which are unpleasant to experience and deal with.

However, the positive side of a Venus Retrograde is healing. Although it is uncomfortable, acceptance, awareness, and healing are your tools during this rough time.

As strong as the urge to run away from your problems, you must be compassionate and brave enough to take this journey head-on. So, avoid running away and begin your healing journey during this time.

Mars

Mars goes into retrograde every twenty-six months and lasts 80 days, meaning that you do not experience it as often as other planetary retrogrades. You experience stagnancy in your sex life, and your energy levels drop significantly. The retrograde may bring up pent-up anger, so you could be angrier than usual during this period.

The best way to deal with Mars retrograde is to find healthy ways to deal with suppressed anger.

It is probably best to avoid acting on impulse or entertaining your aggression. It may be best to sit back, reflect on your feelings, and take time off from starting new projects or setting things into motion. It's time to relax now.

Jupiter

This planet goes retrograde every nine months and remains in this position for approximately four months. During this time, you are more introspective and philosophical. You are most likely to question everything around you. You will look closely at laws, rules, religions, and beliefs instilled within you and never questioned before.

One of the distinctions of this time is that it shakes your blind faith and provokes you to question it. This may be a difficult thing to go through, but Jupiter pushes you to connect with your higher mind and spiritual self.

It may be best to avoid resistance against the planet and open yourself to the universe.

Freeing yourself from false beliefs and exercising self-discipline is encouraged because the retrograde might make you want to self-indulge unhealthily.

Saturn

Saturn retrogrades once every year and stays that way for four and a half months. This time of year is challenging, and you will be learning to face your inner critic. It is tough because inner critics are harsh and difficult to please. You will feel more restricted during this time and face fear-based limitations.

Nobody likes to feel limited, but you must endure this disadvantageous factor of this period. On the other hand, you will come out of this period with more realistic expectations of yourself. You could be more disciplined and patient with yourself after the retrograde is over.

Running away from responsibilities and giving into fear-based limitations are not encouraged during this time.

A better course of action would be coming to terms with your limitations as a human and learning the lesson the planet teaches.

Saturn's lessons are based on the house, sign, and aspects in your natal chart. So, check your birth chart to understand which areas need improvement in your life.

Uranus

Uranus retrogrades every year and stays in this motion for five months. This retrograde may slip the rug from under you—just when things are all right, suddenly, your world is hit by an earthquake. It is a wake-up call reminding your authentic self of the one you may have been repressing.

It may put you in difficult situations to make you confront truths you have been avoiding. As unpleasant as this is, you will need to get out of these situations by sticking to your truth and doing what is best for you.

If the planet pushes you to be yourself, it may put you in situations where your real self is repressed, and you cannot live authentically. Whatever your situation, you'll need to find a way to handle this sudden change with a clear head.

This planet will attempt to free you from the shackles of tradition and old-fashioned thinking and your inauthentic parts. So, during this time, avoid holding onto the safety of the norm and throw yourself into the unknown. The planet will bless you with good outcomes if you let go and trust that you'll be okay.

Neptune

Neptune retrogrades once a year and stays in this phase for approximately six months. Normally, this planet shields you from harsh realities, meaning that when it retrogrades, the veil drops.

This experience can be difficult because you deal with hidden feelings, thoughts, and impulses. A different side of you will rise to the surface, and you will not like it. The planet strips away your denial, and you must face your reality.

The only real benefit of Neptune retrograde is that you deal with undealt realities, whether they are yours or they surround you.

Denial can be very tempting this time of year, but it is vital that you resist this urge. If you resist Neptune's influence, it may severely force you to see the truth. So, it's best to come to terms with your truth.

You may also find yourself attracted to drug use during the retrograde. Enjoying a glass of wine is harmless, but using alcohol to escape is not encouraged during this time. Neptune rules alcohol use, so if you use it to escape, Neptune will ensure the truth follows you until you have dealt with it.

Pluto

Pluto retrogrades once a year and remains in retrograde for five or six months. As mentioned before, Pluto rules everything hidden. So, during its retrograde, you will face things hidden from you or have your secrets exposed.

You may experience disturbing memories or feelings your subconscious has protected you from. They may come to you in dreams, or you may remember them suddenly, but it will not be pleasant either way.

Transformation is needed; however, it can be painful. Unfortunately, Pluto's transformations break you or shatter your whole world. This can be a challenging time, but you should remember that you will soon meet your new, more evolved self. The thought alone can be comforting when life gets dark.

During this time, avoid resisting your transformation. The smart thing to do is to embrace it. Accepting this time of your life can help you be more self-compassionate and go through this period with as much grace as you can.

Observing planetary movements is critical to understanding the current phase you are living in. Sometimes you will find yourself in weird circumstances and do not know why or how you ended up in these situations. Normally, when you question your life because suddenly things feel off, it is most likely caused by planetary movements asking you to make necessary changes.

Chapter 5: Moon Phases and Nodes

The Moon is a powerful celestial body. It mainly harnesses female energy; however, it is not that simple. Every month, the Moon goes through nine different phases, each with a certain energy that affects you differently.

In this chapter, you will learn about the phases in detail and be introduced to their nodes.

The phases of the moon.
https://www.pexels.com/photo/phases-of-the-moon-1983032/

The Lunar Phases

New Moon

The new moon is the first lunar phase in the cycle. You see it right after the dark moon when this luminary body disappears completely. It looks like a tiny sliver of the Moon, which makes sense because it is right when the Moon is between the Earth and the Sun, so, normally, you do not see much of it.

New moon.
https://www.pexels.com/photo/silhouette-of-mountain-under-the-moon-covered-with-clouds-4100130/

This moon symbolizes new beginnings, new chapters, enthusiasm, energy, and motivation, and this phrase carries a lot of energy. It may end a horrible phase in your life, give you some motivation, or bless you with a burst of energy you lack.

You can harness this phase's energy in various ways. For instance, if you have wanted to embark on a project, whether in your personal life or work, now is the time to do so. You can reflect on your life during this time. Ask yourself: What path should I be taking now? Is it time I introduce myself to something new? Should I be exploring a new chapter in my life?

Waxing Crescent

The waxing crescent is the second moon phase and comes two days after the new moon. From its name, you can already tell it looks like a bright silver crescent in the night sky. This is when you see how bright the moon is after two phases of providing little or no light.

Waxing crescent.
https://commons.wikimedia.org/wiki/File:Waxing_crescent_moon.jpg

The waxing crescent symbolizes courage, new opportunities, faith, positivity, and new challenges. It does not influence reckless or impulsive behavior but encourages you to take leaps of trust without overthinking things. It does not want you to be discouraged, so it gives you a little bravery and trust.

During this time, it is ideal for working on your trust. Reflect on the areas you think you lack trust in and face them. Allow yourself to be influenced by the energies the moon offers you. Be braver and speak up. What you have to say is important, and whatever new opportunities come your way now should be considered. Avoid dismissing them out of anxiety and fear. Believe in yourself and the universe.

First Quarter Moon

The first quarter moon is the third phase. It appears a week after the new moon. It looks like a half-bright moon in the sky, which is why it is occasionally referred to as the half-moon.

First quarter moon.
Jim Evans, CC BY-SA 4.0 <https://creativecommons.org/licenses/by-sa/4.0>, via Wikimedia Commons https://commons.wikimedia.org/wiki/File:1st_Quarter_Moon.jpg

If half of the Moon is bright and clear, the other one is dark and hidden—similar to a binary relationship between what you can and cannot see. Therefore, this phase symbolizes strength, focus, commitment, determination, decisive decision-making, and re-evaluation. It could also represent what we can't see, whether inside us or the things beyond us.

At this time of the month, you should thoroughly reevaluate yourself. You can journal your findings to make this process easier. Think about how you have been treating yourself and others. Are you working on your goals one step at a time? Are you avoiding making goals because of fear? Reevaluate the people whom you give your time, energy, and love. Are they worth it? What do they do in return? Commit to enhancing yourself during this time, shed the fear of the unknown, and do not let it hinder your journey.

Gibbous Moon

The gibbous moon comes after the first quarter and right before the full moon, which is an interesting placement. This moon looks like a bright ball in the sky, yet you can't see it all yet.

Gibbous moon.
Opoterser, CC BY 3.0 <https://creativecommons.org/licenses/by/3.0>, via Wikimedia Commons https://commons.wikimedia.org/wiki/File:Gibbous_Moon.jpg

As mentioned, this phase is interesting because it is right before the full moon. So, why is this important? It means that it encourages you to rise to your full potential. It symbolizes development, self-worth, wealth, gains, and manifestation.

During this phase, you can manifest what you want in your life, whether a certain lifestyle, friends, situation, money, or anything else on your mind. After this, you can start thinking about how to develop these areas. If financial security has been troubling you lately, put more effort into finding a passive income or begin an easy side job because the Moon will bless you with gaining whatever you lack during this time.

Also, think about how you can reach your full potential. You may need to work on some skills or discover new things about yourself. You could read more and gain more knowledge. Use the Moon's bright illumination and enlighten your mind with knowledge.

Full Moon

The full moon is the mid-point of the lunar phases. This is as bright as the Moon is going to get. It comes right after the gibbous moon and is not difficult to identify. It is full and bright—so bright that it lights up the whole sky.

Full moon.
Gregory H. Revera, CC BY-SA 3.0 <https://creativecommons.org/licenses/by-sa/3.0>, via Wikimedia Commons https://commons.wikimedia.org/wiki/File:FullMoon2010.jpg

This phase symbolizes abundance, fertility, blooming, emotional times, powerful energy, and healing. This moon is known as one of the most powerful moons. It provides you with ample illumination and enlightenment. Suddenly, everything is clear to you, and understanding or navigating your emotions is no longer difficult.

You may be emotional during this time. Embrace it; do not run away from it. The Moon, after all, rules emotions, so when it is full, it shines a light on your emotions. You can reflect on how you feel and write it down. Think about it or talk about it with your therapist if needed. You may be facing difficult emotions during this time if you are one to run away or hide from them.

Aside from your feelings, you can work on your gratitude. The more grateful you are, the more blessings you will receive from the universe. It is the perfect timing for this since the Moon is providing you with abundance.

Waning Gibbous

The waning moon comes after the full moon when the phases parallel each other. It looks like the gibbous moon, except the shadowy side is on the other side of the gibbous moon.

Waning gibbous moon.
Serge Meunier from Netherlands, CC BY 2.0 <https://creativecommons.org/licenses/by/2.0>, via Wikimedia Commons
https://commons.wikimedia.org/wiki/File:Waning_gibbous_moon_near_last_quarter_-_23_Sept._2016.png

Remember, every phase of the full moon will be about getting rid of something or ending a chapter. When we are approaching the full moon, we are gaining and developing. However, as we move away from it, we start shedding things to begin a new cycle.

This phase symbolizes getting rid of wasteful habits or the things that bring you grief or hinder your progress. This could also be applied to unhealthy thinking or destructive habits, like self-sabotage.

Consider reflecting on the traits or habits you need to shed during this time. Things that you have been unconsciously entertaining. You need to be aware that these things do not serve you anymore, so it is time you get rid of them.

Third-Quarter

The third quarter moon comes after the waning gibbous. It resembles the first quarter moon. When you look up at the sky, you see less and less of the Moon as the cycle comes to an end.

This phase also has a shadow side. Hence, the third quarter symbolizes working on the shadow self. The shadow self contains traits you do not like about yourself, such as things you do that bring you down and do not build you up. By paying attention to this part of yourself, you can eliminate certain toxic traits or behaviors to become a better you.

Shadow work is a big aspect of spirituality. You can learn about this part of you by locating Black Moon Lilith's placement in your natal chart and understanding how it affects you and those around you. Shadow work is not an easy journey to embark on, but it is necessary for self-development.

Waning Crescent

The waning crescent moon appears after the third quarter. Again, it looks like the waxing crescent moon.

This phase symbolizes detachment and isolation. These might be difficult energies; however, they are necessary for your well-being. Staying connected to the world all the time is draining, especially if you have yet to pay attention to your energy levels. Spending time with yourself can reveal many things that need your attention. They could be anything from your feelings, unaddressed thoughts, and self-care.

During this phase, you might tell your friends you will take some time for yourself. Sit with yourself after work, take yourself out on a date, or indulge in any activity you enjoy. You can journal or take notes from a self-help book. There are no rules you need to follow as long as you spend time with yourself and avoid self-neglect.

Dark Moon

The dark moon is the final Moon in the lunar phase. It appears two days before the new moon. You cannot see it because it is barely there. It's almost like it has disappeared from the sky.

This phase symbolizes endings, wisdom, birth, rebirth, secrets, transformation, the release of inner trauma and pain, stillness, and death. Of course, events like death, birth, and rebirth are not literal with this moon phase. They represent the inner cycle you go through when you transform. The old you die, and the new you are rebirthed.

Reflect on the shadow work you have done previously and start shedding the old you during this phase. Going through a transformation phase can be difficult, so be compassionate with yourself throughout this difficult period. Exercise self-love during this time because recognizing your shadow self does not mean you are worthless or not worthy of love.

You may be experiencing fear because you feel you are losing parts of yourself—this is normal. You're losing parts of yourself, but they are those that you need to shed to gain a healthier you.

The Lunar Nodes

The Moon's nodes, also known as the north and south nodes, are two points of intersection around the Moon's orbit when it crosses the eclectic. These nodes play a vital role in Karmic Astrology. Simply, the nodes tell a story of your past life. Both carry information about your karma during this life based on how you led your past life.

Understand that the nodes go hand in hand. You cannot understand the meaning of one without the other. Together they form a complete picture, so you need to understand their positions and meaning together.

☊ North Node

The north node symbolizes the soul's growth. There are things that you lacked or did not experience in your past life. So, your karma in this life is to experience them and grow.

It points to a certain path you will be on during this life, so you must know your north node's location and meaning.

This path is full of rewards for you; however, it may be challenging to go through, like anything in life. So, when you understand what your path is, you will receive divine assistance promised by the north node placement.

Once you understand what you should be doing to reach the apex of success, you must work on yourself. Surely, this path was tailored for you the moment you were birthed. Yet, it was also made for the version of you that is willing to work on itself and has enough self-love and dedication to reach its potential.

The path that is being pointed to may not seem like you. It might point to a direction you did not imagine or never thought of as a possibility. These thoughts and feelings are normal, but trust that the universe has your best interest at heart.

☋ South Node

The south node represents your past, the foundation on which your current life is built. Certain habits and comfort zones within you are from your past lives. You can find yourself reverting to your old ways unconsciously in this life.

Aspects of the south node are important. For example, if you have a conjunction between a planet and the south node, it is time you completely moved on from your past.

You do not need to go through past life regressions or entertain past life memories because they hold no value now.

The south node can tell you a lot about your past life's karma in Karmic Astrology. You can find out about your karmic debt here.

The south node is not a crystal clear picture of who you were. Rather it is a collection of the place you grew up, your struggles, skills, and everything else about you. Through this information, you can learn about your good and bad karma.

Lunar Nodes Placements

To better understand the node's placements, look at this example of breaking down this placement.

The nodes are opposite to each other, naturally. If the north node is in the first house, the south node is in the seventh house.

Per Karmic Astrology, the north node in the first house and the south node in the seventh house means you prioritize your partner and other people close to you more than you prioritize yourself. You give them too much, and there is not enough left for you.

It also means that you feel worthless without a partner. Somehow, you think your partner completes you or is a key element to your survival. This placement says you have made many sacrifices to please your partner and others close to you.

With this placement, the north node is what you need to develop; this is the path you should be on. Developing these traits will free you from your south node karma.

Do not be surprised if you relate to your south node placement. These feelings can still arise in your current life.

☊	1st house	• Develop a healthy sense of self. • Be independent. • Work on healthy boundaries. • Avoid codependent relationships. • Build a strong identity. • Be more self-assured. • Stand up for yourself. • Learn to listen to yourself and don't put too much emphasis on what people have to say or think about you. • Prioritize yourself. • Work on self-love. • Work on abandonment issues. • Address your loneliness and find the root cause.
☋	7th house	• Feelings of worthlessness and inadequacy. • Feeling that you are not enough. • Struggled with self-love and thought you were not worthy of love, kindness, or anyone's attention. • Threatened when someone close leaves your life. • Easily fall into codependent relationships.

Identify the nodes in your birth chart.

Now, it is your turn to decode the nodes' placements.

Follow these steps for an easy interpretation:
1. **Identify their location.**
   Sign and house.
2. **Interpret the lunar node placement based on its location.**
   An easy way is to understand the properties of the sign and house with the nodes.

Understanding your emotions can be a complex and overwhelming task to complete. However, on a more positive note, studying your moon placement, the moon phase you were born under, and how it affects you can give you much insight. The present moon phase also affects your emotions, so observe how you feel under each phase every month to come closer to understanding human emotion's complexities.

You may additionally dedicate some time to studying your nodes to learn about your past and future in this lifetime.

Chapter 6: Astrological Houses

Now that you are familiar with birth charts, the zodiac, planets, and the Moon phases, this chapter explains the twelve astrological houses by listing each house and how you look at your birth chart. Lastly, it provides sign rules to explain to which house each zodiac sign belongs.

Understanding the Houses in Astrology

The birth chart consists of twelve equal sections comprising the houses. These houses differ from the zodiac wheel determined by the Sun's annual rotation. The houses reflect a twenty-four-hour rotation of the Earth around its axis, and the two systems are often combined when astrologers read a birth chart. Make sure you discover the exact time of your birth when you are creating your chart, as the slightest change will make a difference.

The houses in the astrology chart are crucial since they represent different aspects of your life based on your birth location and time. When you plot your chart, these can indicate any challenges you will face or have faced, along with the advantages you have in life.

Do not worry when you first study your chart. If you have some empty areas while others are populated with symbols, that is totally normal. Look first at your ascendant sign, as this is your starting point. Look to the left-most point on your horizon line for the sign that comes from it and applies to your birth.

When you look at the houses, start at the point marked 1 or AC and from the mid-left part of the zodiac wheel. Work anticlockwise on the chart from the first house to the twelfth house. The following are the descriptions of each house that will help you understand how the houses lying in specific signs influence your life.

First House/Ascendant/AC/Rising Sign

The first house, also known as the birth chart ruler, determines how other people perceive or see you. In other words, it is a reflection of yourself to the world. It's the side of yourself that other people view. You must know that the Sun is your sign.

Second House

The second house represents personal wealth, material goods, and self-confidence. It specifically rules everything that involves your financial standing, including liquid assets. It also expresses your feelings toward those assets. The feelings we have for material things drive our motivations when spending money. The second house also shows the career you should follow for good material gains.

Third House

The third house is about communication and how we relate to our siblings, early education, and other aspects like local travel. It determines how you interact with others in different aspects of your life.

Fourth House/Imum Coeli/"Bottom of the Sky"

This area on the chart focuses on things that happen behind the scenes in homes. Some aspects like personal views, traditions, family, and ancestors are personal, and many people don't want to share them with others.

Fifth House

This house depicts elements like casual love affairs, creativity, flirtations, crushes, fun, risks, and entertainment. It guides you in love matters.

Sixth House

The house is about personal health, household pets, daily routine, and coworkers. It is concerned with the things you encounter every day. Often, individuals who belong to this house display a high degree of organization and tend to focus on time management.

Seventh House/Descendent/DC

This house refers to current friends, enemies, and ex-partners. This is part of the area that reflects all relationships and partnerships.

Eighth House

This is a home of transformation, intuition, debt, growth, and power. It is known as the house of sex, death, taboos, and other people's possessions. The house rules other people's money and different possessions. It's also the darkest in the natal chart since it rules death and shows how one will die.

Ninth House

A house of education, the rule of law, traveling a long way, and the meaning of life. The people who belong to the ninth house are usually curious and eager to learn new things. It encourages you to have an open mind and keep a watchful eye on the world around you.

Tenth House/Midheaven/Medium Sky/Medium Coeli

This house shows your image, public standing, or career. It is found at the top of the chart and tells a lot about your unique story. The individuals who belong to this house are ambitious.

Eleventh House

The house explains how you relate with your acquaintances, humanitarian projects, classes, and hopes. The development of humankind dominates this sign, both in the physical world and the ideas surrounding it.

Twelfth House

This house is about our subconscious desires, mental health, punishment, addiction, secret relationships, prison, enemies, magic, and anything hidden from others. The people born in this house are intuitive and psychic.

Interpreting the Houses of Your Birth Chart

Find the ascendant first and look for the houses corresponding to each planet in your chart. You need to understand each planet's function to begin the process.

Once you have the planet pinpointed, study what that planet represents and how that applies to the house it is in—how does the energy display itself? Since each house has a meaning, a close analysis of the chart helps you understand the connection between different houses and the birth chart. The following table highlights the meaning of each house.

House	Meaning
1st House	Self, vitality, appearance, and life force
2nd House	Resources, assets, and self-worth
3rd House	Daily rituals, communication, siblings, and extended family
4th House	Home, foundations, and parents
5th House	Sex, creative energy, and children
6th House	Health and work
7th House	Committed partnerships
8th House	Mental health, death, and other people's resources
9th House	Travel, publishing, education, religion, philosophy, and astrology
10th House	Career and public activities
11th House	Community and good fortune
12th House	Loss, sorrow, and hidden life

Meaning of Astrological Houses

Astrological houses reflect a journey from your immediate self into the world. The first six houses are known as "personal houses" since they focus on self-image, daily habits, values, and ancestry. The other six houses are interpersonal since they focus on partnerships, career opportunities, travel, and the communities we build.

The First House of Self

This represents the main facets of your personality. You can look to this house for your physical representation and the main tenets of your character. Natal planets found in the first house are believed to have an effect on someone's life. For example, Mercury represents a chatterbox in the first house, while the Moon shows someone with high emotions. The first house is the first stop that marks the transition of planets, which means our goals are manifested. This gives birth to new thoughts, creativity, and the ideas needed to shape our world.

The Second House of Possessions

The house of material things, money, and worth. The house also deals with the emotions connected to these things. The house of possessions deals directly with the material, and this reflects security. While it does mainly deal with the physical, it still concerns the mental and spiritual. The house will reflect your own worth, too.

The Third House of Communication

A house of community, communing, and movement. When you utilize this house, you can forge better relationships on a small scale. Communication is vital to building friendships and is a great solution to most problems we encounter in different situations.

The Fourth House of Home and Family

We can look to our immediate surroundings with this house—dealing with our home and familial relationships within it. When we have family around us, we feel safe, secure, and loved. The house extends beyond the physical infrastructure and family bonds to include our pets and any other living beings in our home.

The Fifth House of Pleasure

A childlike house, but only in a positive way. You can find youthful energy, creativity, innocence, and romantic relationships here. If you are looking to express yourself, you can do so through this house. You can also channel this house when you want to feel more joy and happiness in your work, hobbies, or endeavors.

The Sixth House of Health

The house relates to everything to do with health and wellness. If you are looking to exercise, build muscle, or improve your body, you do so through the sixth house. Use this house when you are focusing on your work/life balance, or need to realign yourself when you have been working too hard. This house will help you to better manage your time when you are managing your schedule.

The Seventh House of Partnership

The house of change and relationships. This house includes a lot, which can affect your life in general. Things like lifelong friendships, family homes, finances, and other relationships are reflected here. This house symbolizes things like significant relationships and romantic partnerships in your life. Building strong relationships is important in our lives since it determines how we relate to other people around us. The house will also help with moving to a new job, closing any deal, or signing a contract.

The Eighth House of Sex, Death, and Transformation

The house of major transformations—death being one of them and sex being another—can change a relationship and bring new life into the world. There is also a touch of the supernatural here—another change from the physical to the spiritual—and while the house can be connected to the occult, there is nothing to fear.

You should listen to your desires and channel them appropriately, for death comes for us all. In other words, we must enjoy our short lives. However, the house reminds us to be adaptable and avoid becoming prisoners of the past. You should be ready to embrace the present and future. The planets moving through this house remind us of life's complexities and how we can deal with different situations.

The Ninth House of Philosophy

The house deals with the meaning of life, which comes from more than just philosophy—we need education and a global sense of the world, too. You must look outside who you are and the people around you to see other perspectives and ideas. People with natal planets in the ninth house are curious to know different things in life.

When this house is strong with the planets, you will find that you are more accepting of outside knowledge and may even seek it out—by study or travel. The house can encourage you to expand upon what you know, seeing things as others do not.

The Tenth House of Social Status

This house is at the peak of your birth chart, making it the end of your story—but, of course, your story does not ever end. This house is about what you want for your life—your aspirations, hopes, and dreams for the world. You can focus on this house for your ambition in your personal and professional lives.

The Eleventh House of Friendship

We need more than just work and relationships in life; we also need our friends. When you accomplish something, you must share the joy with someone close to you. The house is associated with our networks and other humanitarian pursuits. This house reminds us to remember our friends who keep us going through difficult situations.

Innovation and technology exist in this zone. If you have a strong connection to this house, you probably have large ideas that can shake the very foundations of our world.

The Twelfth House of the Unconscious

This house deals more with the metaphysical than the known world. Look to this house to help decipher your dreams, emotions, feelings, and other secrets. You may have excellent intuition within this house.

When the planets move through this house, we attract karmic people; however, they also remind us that not all relationships are designed to last. Many things happen in life and affect how we relate to others. The twelfth house is associated with Pisces energy.

Astrological Signs and Their Link to Stars of the Zodiac

Understanding the connection between houses and zodiac signs is vital since houses play crucial roles in our birth charts. Understanding the meaning of different houses helps you know the meanings of each planet and zodiac sign. There are twelve astrological houses and twelve zodiac signs, which are somehow connected. The following are the twelve astrological houses and their corresponding zodiac signs.

Aries: First House

The first house is about you and represents identity, self, appearance, and self-worth. Mars is dominant in this house and helps to drive us forward. That means that Mars also influences Aries.

Taurus: Second House

The house of personal achievement and talents. We can look to Taurus for our values and personal worth. We feel more secure and stable when we focus on this house and sign, and Venus is influential here, too. If you belong to this zodiac sign, you are surrounded by various aspects of dealing with love.

Gemini: Third House

The third house corresponds with Gemini and focuses on communication, mental processes, and intellect. This house focuses on using logic and thinking rationally to make sense. Gemini prioritizes learning in whatever form it comes. If you belong to this house, you must be keen to learn new things and explore the world around you.

Cancer: Fourth House

The fourth house is heavily influenced by the Moon but still dominated by Cancer. Look to this house for indications of family and your home. This is your foundation, your upbringing in the world, and those who have come before you. Cancer is like a string here, the Moon will guide you, and you can look to water signs, too.

Leo: Fifth House

The fifth house is mainly concerned with pleasure and is ruled by the Sun, the source of creativity. It is directly linked to Leo. This house brings a lot of pleasure in many forms—the house will guide your vacations and help with hobbies, pursuits, and children.

Virgo: Sixth House

The house of health, wealth, and daily routines. The aspects that affect your daily routine are affected by this house. Therefore, this house is related to the quality of your work in whatever you do. This house is related to Virgo, who is detail-oriented. If you belong to this zodiac sign, the chances are very high that you have an eye for detail.

Libra: Seventh House

Libra is dominant in the seventh house. This house will rule over many different types of relationships—familial, romantic, and friendships. You can also let it guide you in your business relationships.

Scorpio: Eighth House

The house of Scorpio is rooted in psychology and transformation. Look to this sign when dealing with death, change, or rebirth. This house helps with transitions in all ways—a movement from any stage of your life to another.

Sagittarius: Ninth House

The house of understanding the world on different levels—looking to the bigger questions and traveling to different places to experience different cultures. When you visit new places, you learn things other than what you are used to or comfortable with. Sagittarius rules the ninth house since it is associated with traveling. Sagittarius is also ruled by Jupiter, the planet of wisdom, luck, and travel.

Capricorn: Tenth House

The tenth house concerns status, career, social standing, and reputation. It corresponds with the goal-oriented Capricorn sign and is ruled by Saturn. It is a planet represented by the sea goat.

Aquarius: Eleventh House

The eleventh house is also known as the community house, representing fortune. It deals with hopes, groups, friends, and dreams. If you belong to this house, you will be anxious to achieve your goals. Saturn and Uranus rule the house. The eleventh house is viewed as the representation of the future. Aquarius is the zodiac sign for this house and is mainly concerned with innovation. Aquarius is also concerned about doing things better to make a difference from the popular beliefs held by many people.

Pisces: Twelfth House

The twelfth house, known as the house of secrets, deals with mysticism and seclusion. It is ruled by Pisces. People who belong to this house want to live secret lives. The house is also co-ruled by Neptune and Jupiter.

Astrological houses reflect the life journey you travel and reflect different things you encounter. This chapter explained the meanings of the twelve astrological houses and their implications on the birth chart. The chapter also highlighted the zodiac signs that rule each house and explained the importance of the relationship between the zodiac signs and each house.

Chapter 7: Align with Your Karmic Life Purpose

Finding meaning in life and being purposeful in how we treat ourselves and one another is one of the universe's greatest gifts and also one of its most puzzling mysteries. Humans' so-called search for meaning seems like a cliché, but it is truly at the heart of what drives so many of humanity's endeavors, whether individuals realize it on a practical level or not. However, what do we mean when we say, "karmic life purpose?"

You are probably wondering how it's different from the usual sayings bandied about finding our place in the world and whether our work is purposeful and positively impacts others.

This chapter devotes some time to figuring out precisely how to understand your karmic life purpose and ensure you make the most of the gift provided to you.

Our Distracted Times

We are swamped with information these days. Arguably, information that comes in a deluge is rarely useful and can have the opposite effect. Instead of feeling empowered, you feel overwhelmed and confused. Maybe the information that comes to your phone or computer without context is misinformation, rumors, and lies that do not make much sense but nonetheless leave you feeling hopeless. More than ever, we are distracted by looming wars, an ongoing pandemic, difficult economic circumstances, and empty consumerism—pretty and filtered ads that promise us the world. Yet, the products leave us feeling hollow. Our attention spans are limited and have become even more compressed in response over time because you can only retain so much information. It has made finding our purpose even harder since there's a lot of noise out there about what we should do or how to spend our time to feel productive and worthy of your community's love and respect. Sadly, that worth is sometimes tied to things like your job and salary, the house you can afford, etc. It seems that society has concluded that altruism is for suckers, and unless you join the daily hustle and grind, you are not doing meaningful work.

The messaging for millennials is arguably even more convoluted since the concept of "hustling harder" has been conflated with "doing what you love." Of course, a lot of ink has been wasted on how these disparate concepts have morphed to create much of the solipsism and silly high-mindedness of "dudebros" running Silicon Valley. Thankfully, that phase is coming to an end— partly due to the pandemic and how it has thrown these strange ideas into high relief, exposing them for the empty sloganeering they always were.

To that effect, the so-called "Great Resignation" seems to be a response colored in part by the desire to find some higher purpose, adding a deeply spiritual meaning to what we hope to accomplish on this planet before leaving it. We are still distracted by everything around us, and these are exceptionally difficult times, with good reason. However, more and more people are cutting through the sadness and despair, the capitalistic ideals of what a good person entails, and doing something that feeds their soul and helps others feel loved and safe. For centuries, humankind was largely devoted to understanding the concept of "purpose" and discovering its meaning. That philosophizing seems to have died out, and there are not as many active philosophers today whose words are consumed in the same manner as they were in the last century.

Nonetheless, despite the constant noise around us, the issue has come up again, piercing the cloud of frustration and hounding so many people. Now, people are trying to understand the karmic life's purpose and how to find theirs. Having a central purpose has helped many people live long and healthy lives for years because they feel they have something tangible to live for, a central purpose. Without it, we would feel lost and unmoored. In this deeply individualistic society, it could be heresy to say that you want to live for something other than yourself.

Still, it is a risk worth taking since it will make you feel more grounded and hopeful about the world around you in the long run.

Definitions

Earlier in this book, some content was devoted to exploring the meaning of karma and how it can be applied to everyday life. As previously mentioned, karma is Sanskrit for action or deed, but spiritually it refers to the principle of cause and effect. We hear this as part of various daily phrases, explaining how karma is a... well, you know the rest. Yet that is a rather tidy and not wholly truthful definition of the word.

Karma, in principle, means focusing your intentions so they influence the world around you. Hence, if you are concerned with putting good karma out there, you should expect better karma in return—not necessarily in this life, but perhaps in the next or reincarnation. Of course, bad intentions often go hand in hand with bad deeds and will contribute to bad things coming your way. Again, that does not mean you will reap the consequences immediately—perhaps later in life or through your rebirth. For most Indian religions, karma is deeply tied to the idea of rebirth. It is in stark contrast to how the principle has been adopted in the West, wherein consequences are thought to occur here and now and not on another metaphysical plane of existence.

Now, with that refresher out of the way, it is time to pay attention to what we mean by "life's purpose" and how it is connected with the principle of karma. The first part of this chapter explained the meaning of life and humankind's search for it more generally. However, finding a spiritual purpose is slightly different from finding meaning in life—although they are somewhat linked. In truth, finding a spiritual purpose is more about becoming a better version of yourself and perhaps finding fulfilling and meaningful work, as those behind the Great Resignation will tell you—although work is one part of the equation. How we move in all areas of our lives and how we treat ourselves and others is at stake when we define this term in a spiritual sense.

It has become very easy to feel disconnected from our communities, ourselves, and our spiritual way of life. The disenchantment with organized religion has only compounded this problem, causing people to splinter into different isolated groups since they do not see themselves represented in any of the hallowed realms of mainstream religions. It can be argued that humankind's natural state is to have a deep core of spirituality at its center, and having that torn away is one of the modern tragedies of everyday life. There are many understandable reasons for this, but it is worth underscoring that finding time for personal reflection and practicing different spiritual wellness is good for the individual and the community. It allows us to harness the energy required to fight many of the injustices we see in the world. Without our spirituality, the desire to fight for what is right can be significantly weakened.

Moreover, finding and cultivating your karmic life purpose can and should be its reward. No one does it to gain anything in return. If they do, they are truly going about it in the wrong way and will be more spiritually poisoned than the rest of us who go about our days feeling numb. No one should simply exhibit signs of their spirituality but act on it privately. Seeking this purpose means you will be gracious and compassionate and strive toward self-actualization—without trying to hijack others' trauma. It also means you will work on your self-esteem and flourish in your personal relationships. For example, your circle of friends could be small; however, they include healthy relationships with proper boundaries.

Furthermore, a karmic life purpose is completely divorced from material concerns. Take your career out of the equation—unless we are talking about the specific circumstances in which your labor feels toxic or is actively harming the planet in alarming ways. In that case, it will help to eventually consider leaving your full-time job and finding something else that allows you to feel spiritually whole. Generally, material pursuits are not part of the deal here, but they can be connected. A karmic spiritual purpose is more aligned with establishing and implementing a set of values in your daily life. These guiding principles help give your life meaning and inevitably influence your decisions.

Aligning Your Karmic Life Purpose

The words "alignment" and "karma" evoke a new age, hapless approach to life that sounds too woo-woo for most people to employ or even contemplate. It brings up imagery of astrologers and palm readers—both legitimate professions but ones that do not necessarily curry favor with the majority. Also, some ideas behind living a purposeful life may seem cost-prohibitive to many people, and this imagery shrouds much of the work in the guise of elitism that is difficult to shake. Thankfully, there are different ways you can be aligned with your karmic purpose and feel part of a larger community, many of which are modest interventions that don't take up much of your time or resources.

Interestingly, millennials were always recognized as a generation with less brand loyalty than previous generations. Companies soon figured out that the way to gain their trust was to uphold an underlying cause or message behind their product. It is not to say that previous generations were not interested in finding some life purpose and ensuring that their consumer habits reflected as much—we are generally not fans of generalizations. However, it seems that the more our society relies on technology and myths around office work and productivity, the more likely younger generations will throw these concepts into question. They learned that exercising their market power was one way to feel purposeful about how they choose to live their lives. Well, there are other, more in-depth ways to align your karmic purpose, far from the pressure corporations exert on your pocketbook and conscience.

Firstly, sometimes being aligned with your karmic life purpose means allowing yourself to feel vulnerable. Brene Brown has done a great deal of research on the topic and has destigmatized the feeling of being open with others since that has often been mistaken for weakness. If you truly want something, give your heart and soul to that ideal without expectation. Furthermore, never feel detached from the spiritual work you are doing—letting yourself love and serve others while allowing them to nurture that feeling in return is key to a sense of self-worth and purpose. To become a giving person, you must be willing to receive. Trust is built on a willingness to be open, and people will not necessarily feel safe with someone determined to be closed off or unwilling to receive gratitude themselves.

It means that you should also be yourself and never be fake. Sure, keeping boundaries in place is healthy, but don't pretend to be someone you're not. Living in fear of who you are or other people's judgment will only exacerbate the feeling that you're ultimately unable to fulfill your life purpose. This may take a certain measure of courage for many of us since being honest about who you are and what you're about is not always safe or something the surrounding community may encourage. However, authenticity is part and parcel of much of the work that needs to be done here, and you will feel miserable if you're in a situation requiring you to be inauthentic or closed off to others. Living life truthfully allows you to be more open and feel more empathy for others, which, in turn, impacts how you connect with people around you.

Another way to align with your karmic purpose is always to be willing to extend a helping hand. If you can help in some way, don't hesitate. Perhaps you cannot help financially, but maybe you can help others simply by being kind, offering a shoulder to cry on, or listening to other people's concerns. Don't be judgmental or overly ideological. That seems like a tall order in our hyper-polarized world, but it does not have to be. If there is one thing you can do that can benefit others, it is to help out whenever possible. Also, always give to others without expecting anything in return.

This ties into our next point, which is to be friendly. A smile can go a long way, and spreading joy as opposed to a constant stream of negativity is always appreciated. The more good karma you put out into the universe, the more at peace you will feel. Holding onto anger and resentment without a proper outlet could make life even more difficult for you, so it helps to change your perspective slightly and be more open and loving with the universe.

Meditating daily, if only for five minutes at a time, is bound to help you feel calmer and put together, especially during difficult times. Your soul needs time to heal, and the same can be said for almost everyone these days. Meditation is arguably the only time during the day that will allow you to feel grounded and safe in your body as you work to calm yourself and feel prepared for the day ahead. If you are so inclined, try prayer since it similarly helps connect you to the universe on a deeper level. These practices are as old as time and have served a purpose for many years. Many people have benefited from meditation and the like, and it helps to remember that these are tools you can keep in your toolbox as you embark on this journey.

Given how exhausting everything feels these days, you may feel burnout and despondent. Of course, this seems to be the case with many people, and it has become part of an ongoing mental health crisis. If you're wondering how to break the cycle, one thing you can do is explore new ways of developing your creativity. Imagination is usually tapered down due to the pressures of modern life. We have to earn a living, pay off debt, and take care of our sanity in the face of an incredibly insane world. Naturally, your creativity dies amid all of this, making you feel disconnected from the people around you. Creativity isn't only about enjoying or producing arts and crafts; it's about opening yourself up to different experiences and feelings, which is key to achieving a karmic life purpose. If this sounds like you, it's okay to take some time for yourself and let your mind wander.

Alternatively, you could journal for a few minutes every day. Even if you can't afford to do so for half an hour, five minutes of simply writing down your thoughts, feelings, and observations will eventually help you unlock whatever is getting in the way. Your imagination will start to thrive again. Maybe go to a museum one day, bike to your local park, and quietly take notes of what you see. Adding a healthy dose of creativity to your life will eventually open you up to other possibilities or opportunities you may have missed entirely. This hard work will bring you into a deeper alignment with your purpose.

Think of it this way. As a kid, you were probably happy to explore new ideas and could not wait to learn something new. Stories, finger painting, watching a great movie, and playtime with friends were all activities that encouraged a sense of wonder and fondness for the universe at large. As we get older, we forget this sense of wonder, which becomes buried by the effort of simply having to live and care for ourselves in a tiresome world. Once you rediscover the things that previously brought you joy as a child, you may become more vulnerable and excited about aligning with your karmic purpose and making better sense of the world.

Reflections

There are many ways to help you feel aligned with your karmic purpose, and you can do a lot of important work to help you fulfill that endeavor. Ultimately, it is part of a quest that may take up your entire life, and your purpose may change as you evolve. So, before implementing any changes in your life, you need to ask yourself a few questions to help you achieve an enhanced spirituality. Take the following quiz to help guide you and figure out whether or not you are aligned with your karmic life purpose:

1. What is the central purpose that informs my life?
2. I want to be a good person—how should that be defined?
3. Am I connecting with the people in my life? Are there ways in which I can form stronger bonds with the people I care about?
4. Is my day job aligned with what I hope to do in life? Does it help produce impactful helpful work, or does it actively harm others, the environment, etc.?

5. Am I living in the best way possible, or are there blind spots that need to be filled?

Jot down your answers to each of these questions. Take the time to think and mull over precisely what you hope to achieve in life. Honestly, gauge where you are, and note the things you are willing to change or different approaches you can implement. Practicing empathy, compassion, and willingness to be vulnerable is not easy and can take a long time to achieve. Putting pen to paper and being more mindful of yourself and the world around you is an important step in the right direction.

Chapter 8: Understanding and Integrating Karmic Lessons

Karmic cycles are patterns of feelings, emotions, situations, and realizations that you experience repetitively throughout your life. They present themselves as opportunities to unlock a higher level of consciousness or wisdom and ultimately break negative cycles in your life. Karmic lessons will keep repeating themselves until you have finally understood and mastered the lesson at hand so that you avoid the same pitfalls time and time again.

Practitioners of New Age or Indian spirituality, yoga, and astrology are at least familiar with the term Karmic lessons (or cycles). However, this concept may seem rather foreign for those new to the world of spirituality and healing practice. Regardless of your level of expertise, grasping a deeper understanding of the concepts of karma and karmic lessons is necessary if you want to embark on your healing journey.

As you may have guessed, the idea of karmic lessons and cycles initially sprouts from the concept of karma. As you may recall from Chapter One, karma, as a concept, is the essence of numerous Indian religions like Buddhism, Hinduism, Sikhism, and Jainism. When mentioned in a spiritual context, the word typically means something greater than its literal meaning. Karma is a large part of our lives. It focuses on our actions and intentions. Even if we think of an act and do not carry it out, karma still works through that, so it is important to think good thoughts as well as do good deeds.

Thinking positive thoughts can bring about positive outcomes. On the other hand, bad actions and intentions create bad karma, resulting in negative outcomes. Those with positive intentions, who take actions with unintentionally negative outcomes, can create good karma for themselves. In other words, "What goes around, comes around."

Reincarnation and Karmic Cycles

You are probably familiar with the concept of reincarnation in Eastern religions. According to theology, we have all lived several lifetimes, each granting us a chance to grow and work on ourselves for the better. Unfortunately, growth cannot happen overnight. It takes time, effort, and change to become the best versions of ourselves. We must emerge successfully from a series of spiritual, ethical, and moral challenges, otherwise known as karmic cycles.

The experiences, events, and situations we could not deal with correctly during our previous lifetimes take the shape of karmic lessons. We must learn our intended lessons, whether we've failed to put energies into their best use, overcome certain obstacles, made the wrong choices, or discarded potentially life-changing opportunities. Until we do so, these learning opportunities will keep presenting themselves. Once we master the lessons, our life experiences become easier to manage, and we are generally much happier and more joyful. Let us say that you failed to manage a moral challenge in a past lifetime, where societal pressures, fear, or even a lack of knowledge caused you to act contradictory to your morals. A karmic cycle will present similar challenges to you in your current lifetime. These dilemmas appear in your life's professional, familial, romantic, or societal aspects.

In this chapter, you will learn more about karmic lessons and cycles and what you can learn from them. Here, you will come across the signs accompanying karmic lessons to help you identify whether you're experiencing one. Finally, you will learn how to integrate these lessons into your life.

What Can I Learn from a Karmic Cycle?

You may wonder how learning from something you do not remember doing will benefit you. What good will it do if you're forced to learn from situations that a previous reincarnation of yourself mishandled or issues left unresolved for lifetimes?

Well, karmic cycles are typically intended to teach you three main lessons: Staying in touch with your morals and values, staying true to yourself, and trusting the journey. Karmic lessons aim to teach you your role in certain life situations. The main point is to learn to take full responsibility for your actions, behaviors, thoughts, and emotions.

Once you have mastered a karmic lesson, you will realize you're the only person who can walk your unique path in life. No one will be coming in to push you, motivate you, or help you find happiness. It is up to you to use your intuition, harness your strength, work on self-development, and seek happiness. You're meant to be independent and transparent. Living your truth is the only way to break the cycle and take on the challenge. These challenges are not easy to emerge triumphantly. If they were, you would not still be facing them in this lifetime. Instead of resenting or denying the need to learn, you must accept that you are destined to learn and grow from these obstacles. Humbling yourself and embracing those karmic cycles is the key to approaching these lessons with honor. You must garner your inner strength and believe in your ability to grow to succeed.

Signs You're Experiencing a Karmic Lesson

Every step we take in life, whether positive or negative, has an outcome and leads to a consequence. So, there is always a lesson to be learned. Good deeds come with immediate positive consequences that urge us to do more of this good action. On the other hand, negative outcomes are often harder to learn, particularly because very few people realize they are experiencing a karmic lesson. Fortunately, some signs are there to help you determine whether there's a life lesson to be learned.

Things Feel Oddly Familiar

The easiest way to determine whether you are experiencing a karmic lesson is to look for patterns. If you're experiencing a karmic cycle, you will probably feel like your life events revolve around the same themes. Take a moment to think about the problems you face in different aspects of your life, whether in your career, relationship, or family. Do you have stagnant energy when these problems arise?

Perhaps your partner reminds you of a toxic parent, or you constantly find yourself stuck in detrimental work environments. Maybe your destructive cycle creates the same unhealthy environment you grew up in. Do you find yourself chugging on alcohol every night as your father did?

Detrimental cycles and patterns are not purely spiritual. According to psychology, generational and childhood traumas and personal attachment styles can lead to unhelpful behavioral loops. These loops are what we refer to as karmic cycles in spirituality. We must identify the patterns, learn their triggers, and trace them back to a cause to break the cycle.

You Lack Control

How often do you feel like you have no control over your life or at least some aspects of it? You try your best to go down a certain path or make what you think is the right choice. However, going according to plan becomes nearly impossible, and you have to go the other way. Karmic lessons leave you with no choices. They force you to go in a certain direction, even if it is the opposite of what you want, because they want you to see the full picture. In most cases, a karmic lesson will force you to see something you're unaware of.

Things do not always work out. However, if you notice this becoming a pattern, you need to take a step back and ask yourself where you went wrong because this is karma in action.

You're Stuck in a Karmic Relationship

When a karmic lesson is in the works, you will encounter a person you believe you cannot live without. At first, everything will feel like a dream. You'll feel you are destined to be together. However, your hopes and dreams about the relationship started falling apart shortly after. At one point, saving the relationship becomes impossible, no matter how hard you try to patch things up. You'll still hope and try to work things out even then because you cannot help but think your life will be over once that person leaves. Karma will test you by continuously sending this person into your life until you have finally learned your lesson.

You Always Attract Similar People

Whether it's a friend or a romantic partner, think about the people you attract into your life. Do all partners share similar traits? Perhaps your current significant other shares your father's controlling tendencies or your mother's manipulative ways. Psychology reveals that we are naturally drawn toward people, situations, and even emotions that make us feel comfortable, even when they always lead us to the same traumatic cycle. We are attracted to the familiar even when it hurts.

If you grew up in an environment where anger issues were a major concern, the feeling you get, no matter how bad, is incredibly familiar when you see your partner getting angry. So, you tolerate it even when it brings you pain. If you grew up with parents who didn't fulfill your emotional needs, you might feel the most comfortable in relationships lacking emotional intimacy, those that make you feel lonely.

You're Always Facing Your Fears

Have you noticed that most situations you find yourself in bring out at least a couple of your worst fears? Do these events make you wonder whether you'll actually make it out alive? You can't seem to shut down your thoughts to the point where you have to experience multiple sleepless nights. No solution seems viable enough to get you out of this mess. Unless you pinpoint the lesson at hand and master it, you cannot find a solution.

Let us take financial insecurity as an example. Suppose your mind is often preoccupied with monetary problems. In that case, you could end up settling for jobs that bring you no happiness or emotional fulfillment for years just to guarantee stability and financial security. At the same time, you can't shake away visions of your dream job in your mind.

If you're continuously facing problems in your current job or even lose it, this is a karmic opportunity presenting itself. You have two choices: Search for other jobs that promise financial security but lack emotional fulfillment, or take a leap of faith and do what you've always wanted to do. Unless you make the latter choice and face your fears, you will remain stuck in the same karmic cycle. As mentioned above, karmic cycles teach you to garner the strength and courage to be true to yourself. You must always think of these events as opportunities to re-evaluate your choices, current life situation, and desires.

It Feels Your Loved Ones Are Turning against You

If you're still persistent in keeping the lesson unlearned, karma will take drastic measures to ensure you break your cycle. You must know it's time to take the reins and change things around when you feel those closest to you are turning against you. Whether your partner acts impulsively or your best friend acts irrationally, you feel compelled to act unlike yourself. Going against your true nature and doing things you would not normally do indicates a lesson to be learned.

Your Darkest Side Seems to Be Making Its Way Out

We are not typically fully aware of how we react in certain situations unless we experience them. Most of the time, we aren't aware of the extent or extremity of our reactions. Unfortunately, karmic lessons have a way of pushing us to the edge. They keep pressuring us until we lash out, causing the most undesirable, spiteful, and unfavorable traits to surface. It can be a side of you that you never even knew existed.

Karmic Lessons Are a Gateway to Healing

A karmic cycle makes its way into your life to help you attain a higher level of consciousness—ultimately, one that accompanies a greater level of moral and ethical judgment in your current lifetime. Believe it or not, karmic lessons are primarily meant to help you heal. They can be very painful to endure. However, once you overcome them, you'll emerge much stronger, wiser, and more independent. These lessons are meant to help you unlock your full potential and become a better version of yourself. You take major steps toward achieving wholeness once you decide to work on the mental, spiritual, and emotional aspects of your being. With this effort, you'll self-actualize and heal yourself on a much deeper level.

This journey is not easy to tackle on your own. So, we recommend reaching out to a mental health professional (one who respects your spiritual beliefs, of course) to point you in the right direction. A mental health professional can help you point out troublesome patterns more easily. They also help you determine where they come from, what triggers them, and why it's so hard for you to break these cycles. It's important to understand that doing this therapy can be distressing. It's also very hard to get out of your comfort zone and make different choices. Having a professional by your side will provide much-needed support when things get rough. You should also consider holistic therapy since it focuses on optimizing your physical, emotional, spiritual, and mental health.

Things to Keep in Mind

Whether you choose to walk this path on your own or seek help, you must always focus on your relationship with yourself throughout this process. Try your best to practice self-compassion and avoid being overly critical of yourself. Make it your priority to unleash your authentic self and align with your values. Making it to the other side of a karmic lesson is very challenging. Continuously developing the connection with your authentic, most genuine self will give you strength. However, it can increase your chances of breaking these detrimental cycles.

You can change your life just by bringing a karmic cycle to an end. All you need are the right actions, intentions, support, and, most importantly, perspective. Hopefully, you will notice a gradual positive shift in your life circumstances over time. It helps to keep in mind that the essence of karmic lessons extends beyond lifetimes. Once you break free from the loops holding you back, working toward personal growth and development becomes a lot easier. You'll notice your career, lifestyle, and romantic and social relationships elevating in the process.

It is not enough to merely acknowledge that you are experiencing a karmic cycle you need to break. It's no more than one step toward creating change, and learning your lesson is half the equation. You must integrate what you learned into your life to heal fully.

Breaking a Karmic Cycle

To break a karmic cycle, you should be able to recognize it first. Take a moment to reflect on the problematic areas of your life and note any signs mentioned above. Analyze your personal relationships and understand why you feel stuck in this cycle. It will help you determine what lessons you need to learn.

Practicing self-compassion and acceptance is also vital when breaking a karmic cycle. One of the most important things a karmic lesson will teach you is that you must always prioritize your needs in any relationship or situation. Often, we fail to voice our wants and concerns, fearing we may hurt others. Unfortunately, this causes us to push our values, beliefs, and convictions aside.

You can only overcome a karmic lesson by trusting your intuition. Only then will you precisely know what you expect and deserve in any relationship. Your intuition is never wrong, so trust it to guide you to the right path. Breaking a karmic cycle can be broken down into the following five steps.

How to Integrate Your Karmic Lesson

1. Get in Touch with Your Values

Problems will always happen when you are not yourself or not aligning with your values. It is easier to push everything we stand for aside just so we can please the community, make friends, or avoid unnecessary arguments. However, you must take full responsibility for your authentic self, actions, beliefs, behaviors, and thoughts to unlock your full potential.

2. Be Self-Compassionate

We are our worst enemies. Nothing holds us back more than that loud, demanding, and critical voice inside our minds. How do you expect to move forward or work toward personal growth and development when you constantly doubt your abilities? Practicing self-compassion and working toward self-love helps you integrate your karmic lessons. When you're self-compassionate, you learn to trust yourself, your faith increases, and so does your strength. Without self-compassion, you will continue to settle for less.

3. Live for No One Else but Yourself

We all fall into the trap of caring about what others think of us before we take any steps forward. We worry about letting others down or disappointing them even when we are doing what is best for us. We let others determine our path and listen to the advice of others because we doubt our choices. Sometimes, you need to take a step back and realize you're the only person who can decide what's best on your journey. You need to start searching for your own happiness.

4. Lean into Your Intuition and Work on Your Independence

Learning to listen to your intuition and maintaining your independence is the only way you'll fall in tune with your truth. You cannot be your true self if you do not trust yourself or depend on others for direction.

5. Trust the Journey

As explained above, you must embrace that you are destined to learn your karmic lesson. The process is not easy. However, you should not stress because everything unfolds the way it should.

Breaking a karmic cycle requires you to make many significant and uncomfortable changes in your life. Taking these drastic measures isn't easy to tolerate, especially when you may feel compelled to avoid your problems and go back to your old ways. However, it helps to remember the pain that comes with avoiding emotional aspects. Experiencing these karmic cycles over and over is much worse than facing your fears and putting an end to the lesson once and for all.

Chapter 9: Astrological Predictions

A common misconception is that astrology is a new age concept with no bearing in reality or that a mystic practice is more akin to fortune-telling than anything else. This is not a half-truth but rather a flat-out lie obfuscating that true astrology is based on several scientific disciplines and mystical principles. The practice is a complicated exploration of the solar system and how our personalities and life trajectories are tied to the universe. Of course, plenty of bad astrologers out there have contributed to the study's bad name. People writing horoscopes in the vast majority of newspapers and magazines are the same ones who write dodgy messages for fortune cookies from their cramped at-home offices. However, professional astrologers are a different breed, and many are good at what they do and take their work very seriously. Part of that work is using astrology to determine predictions helpful to their clients. Some of the tools they use are complicated and particularly involved, but it is possible to make astrological predictions on your own, provided you have a few basic concepts nailed down. This chapter will help make this work feel more accessible and provide you with a few vital tools that will make it much easier to get the benefits of astrological predictions yourself.

How Astrological Predictions Work

In the simplest terms, astrology is the study of the movements and positions of celestial bodies—the stars and planets—and how they are interpreted in their capacity to influence human life and the natural world. The practice of astrology holds that many answers people look for can be found by simply looking up and making notes of the sky. The word prediction means forecasting a particular event or occurrence. In this sense, it is more about checking something like the weather forecast instead of looking into a crystal ball and telling the future. A prediction is just that—a forecast and nothing more. People conflate what an astrological prediction entails, but the reality is something far more grounded than what appears in mainstream books or television shows. An astrological prediction is a way of finding your way through the fog, and if it suddenly rains, well, at least you are prepared.

So, an astrological prediction definitely does not provide you with knowledge of the future. Rather, it presents a series of guideposts to help you better understand certain situations and how best to react or decide according to the context. For example, a popular astrological prediction is a horoscope. Astrologers typically write these—well, the good ones—and they are presented according to the sun signs. It's nothing more complicated than that. Most legit horoscopes are presented monthly rather than weekly and give you vague ideas on how certain events will make you feel.

Let us say you're an Aquarius. A sample horoscope may read something like this:

These days you find yourself distracted by a wide array of wonderfully compelling people, places, and concepts. They provide a tangible way of distancing yourself from your emotional needs, which can be convenient. Since you're not the type that enjoys being terribly introspective, you could find yourself using most of your energies to connect with others rather than focus on your interior life. That is all well and good, but remember, you should be as generous and non-judgmental of yourself as you are of others. Doing some thinking and taking care of your needs doesn't mean you're selfish. Work to shift your perspective, and note that you are just as worthy of respect and intellectual curiosity as everyone else.

This kind of horoscope writing may seem familiar to you. Much advice is in the realm of the conceptual, and precious little has anything to do with something concrete happening to you at the moment. However, if you take the horoscope for what it's worth, you will realize that much of this seemingly general advice is probably something you could listen to at the moment. That is the thing: Astrological predictions can take the form of advice and offer guidance on how to deal with things you are struggling with. An astrological prediction, be it a horoscope or anything else, is not like something out of a playbook by Nostradamus, e.g., "The universe will end in the year 2000." Of course, Nostradamus was a talented astrologer; however, his predictions have sometimes been taken out of context or misinterpreted by the powers that be to denote other things he probably did not intend to bring into the popular conversation. The point is that a prediction is rarely—if ever—a way to tell you what will happen tomorrow, next week, or the following year. They are bits of information based on your sun sign and the planetary movements in the sky, offering you spiritual guidance to help better make sense of where your life is at.

How to Make Astrological Predictions

Providing a forecast of the future is no easy feat, and it is usually based on very precise tools astrologers use to decipher what their clients should expect in the coming months. Several techniques are used to make an astrological prediction, some of which are based on transits, progressions, and returns.

Before we get into these techniques in-depth, it helps to uncover the tools typically used in drafting astrological predictions in the first place. For one, you will need an ephemeris. In the practice of astronomy and understanding of celestial navigation, an ephemeris is a book that contains tables providing you with the trajectory of naturally occurring astronomical objects, and even artificial satellites in the sky, over a particular period. Some books cover enough information to last a few years; however, most are devoted to making things tangible for hundreds of years at a time. An ephemeris is required for spacecraft making their way to a mission in outer space, but astrologers also use it to help navigate the complex realities of the stars and planets as they relate to sun and moon signs. They are a key part of any serious astrologer's toolkit in understanding how to make an astrological prediction for themselves or others.

The next thing you need, arguably the most important tool in your arsenal, is a birth chart. A natal or birth chart shows the placement of the planets when you were born. That placement helps you to understand who you are and the journey you are on. You will need your date of birth, the location, and the exact time you were born to create a birth chart. If you are unsure of the time, choose an estimate or start at twelve noon. Then, draw the planets and the houses. If this seems too complex, use an online free birth chart template, which will have the correct information for you.

The birth chart will ultimately look like a twelve-slice pie. Each slice is referred to as a house. Each house is associated with a sign of the zodiac. And each zodiac influences your life. The sections in the middle are called aspects and depict how natal planets in your chart communicate with one another. For example, you may have a Taurus sun sign, but your moon sign is Pisces, and your rising sign is Leo. Each informs different parts of your personality and provides important signposts for how different aspects of your life will play out. Each aspect will have a different shape, line, and color and come together at various intersecting points. Depending on the thickness of the line, you can understand how strong a particular connection will be and what to infer from that based on other pieces of information you have on hand.

To read a birth chart, you need to look at three things in unison: Each planet and its concurrent sun sign, the house the planet resides in, and the connections each planet makes with other planets. This information will reveal intricate details about who you are, your fears, strengths, family, childhood, etc.

This now brings us to the techniques mentioned earlier and how they make astrological predictions. Transits are perhaps the easiest to understand of the three complex techniques. If you want to predict what will happen to someone on a given day, all you do is compare the positions of the planets in the sky to their positions in their birth chart. So, the position of the planets moving in the sky is called transiting planets. If your birth chart reads that Pluto is at twenty degrees of Aquarius and transiting Venus, it means that today is a Pluto-Venus day for you, which could be a good time to relax at home and do some gardening, cooking, etc.

Progressions are a bit trickier; however, they function slightly similarly. An astrologer uses different progressions, but the most common is a day for a year progression, sometimes referred to as a secondary progression. This progression is calculated by adding one day to the date of birth for each year of the person's life. This technique allows you to look to the future, maybe ten years from now, and read what the secondary chart predicts will happen at that time. Perhaps there will be a major milestone or the unfurling of a romantic relationship.

Other progressions astrologers use could be the day for a month or tertiary progression. This progress chart adds to the date of birth for each month of life. There is also the solar arc direction, which is not used as often given its complexity, but astrologers also refer to it for guidance. It entails looking at the planets, how they move or rotate within the solar system, and how that pertains to the information on a birth chart.

The last popular technique in astrological prediction is the return. This marks when a transiting planet returns to its position at birth. So, if your sun position is twelve degrees and fifteen minutes of Cancer, the Sun will return to the same position every year around your birthday. Based on this information, a chart is created and used to foretell various issues you need to be mindful of annually. Likewise, the Moon should return to the same position at birth every month, and a chart created for this purpose is referred to as a lunar return chart. This technique pays homage to how certain elements of our life trajectory are circular and part and parcel of the same package, time and again.

Decoding Planetary Transits

For this section and easier digestion, let us briefly go back to the easier concept—astrological transits, and how they help inform your birth chart. The following is a sample of how it could look:

Planets: Venus, Pluto, Jupiter

Natal: 7 - 2

Rules: 9 - 3,8

Moon: 56 - 24

Sun: 4 - 3,1

Of course, this is just the beginning of the work, and you will come across different iterations you need to jot down as you move to the chart. Again, most charts are fairly complicated, so compare various online resources with the templates clearly set out for you. You need to enter some basic biographical data about yourself, and then you can move forward based on what has already been provided. One helpful thing about inputting this data online is that you can also run the birth and transit chart and search for a specific future date to determine what you may encounter at that point in time. An ephemeris is also helpful since it provides a more detailed account of the daily planetary movements and when planets are leaving a specific transit. In layperson's terms, when the planetary return will put the planet's position in the same position as it was at your birth.

This is all fairly complicated, and looking at the wheel of your birth chart can be overwhelming. However, if you take the time to look closely at what each piece of information is telling you, you will eventually know how to crack the codes the universe sets out for each of us at our birth. Astrology is a complex science, and you must also have a strong grasp of astronomy and some of the more mystical branches of religion and psychic studies to have a holistic view of what a chart is telling you. Generally, you can learn a great deal by making a few simple interventions and using a birth chart to your advantage. Luckily, many online resources are making more of these underpinnings accessible and digestible beyond the book in your hands.

Furthermore, much of this work is about practicing. Once you have studied the planets and houses and understood each sign's characteristics, you can pull out an ephemeris and sketch different ideas to help you better navigate how the solar system speaks to your experiences and personality traits. The birth chart is the carrier of so many secrets, and in that sense, you can decode different aspects of your life and figure out astrological predictions that make the most sense to you.

People have turned to astrology to predict the future for a millennium. Following celestial patterns and movements in the sky is a precise technique that requires the practitioner to exhibit great compassion and responsibility. Whether you make predictions for yourself or others, you need a detail-oriented approach to the art form. Sometimes, our obsession with predictions reveals more about our anxieties than anything else, and it is important to acknowledge that dissonance as you make astrological predictions.

If you think that ethical concerns around astrological predictions are overblown, consider this: For a long while, rulers of empires have historically relied upon astrologers as a way of maintaining their power. If the astrologer communicated unfavorable information, many were imprisoned or even killed. So, the ability to bring a certain level of precision and care into the practice of astrology is important and often referred to as a necessity.

Furthermore, people think that making astrological predictions will tell you what will happen in the future and possibly even provide tips on avoiding horrific events. Well, astrology does not result in pat resolutions. In reality, you would be better off thinking about astrology as making forecasts rather than predictions. The main difference is that astrology allows for a more thematic and interpretive guide to reading what might happen in the future. In this sense, horoscopes are a good example since they provide an idea of what could happen to you according to your sun sign, but they will not say something as straightforward as, "Someone will propose to you on May twenty-first."

It's worth remembering that regardless of how precise the work behind astrology is, the astrological prediction will not help you predict a future event or anything concrete. Rather, it provides a general idea of when to expect a major milestone and guidance on handling it depending on your personality traits and history. You would be setting expectations for yourself and others about dealing with different issues and plan to move forward from there. Always remember that the concept of free will is at play, and merely because something happens to you doesn't mean that you need to go through with it or not work to alter the lead-up to that event. The decision is ultimately yours, and you can make the right one depending on the information.

Chapter 10: Reincarnation — The Law of Karmic Return

Reading this book, you are likely to have already encountered the idea of reincarnation and the law of karmic return. However, while other chapters touched on this concept momentarily, you should be know much more concerning these two ideas.

If you're struggling with understanding how karma and reincarnation are tied together and what the law of karmic return means, do not worry—you're in the right place. This chapter will cover everything you need to know and give you a chance to re-test how good your karma is to see how you have changed by reading and following this book.

Understanding Reincarnation and the Law of Karmic Return

Before you understand how karma and reincarnation are tied together, you will first need to understand what these ideas mean beyond the definition of the two terms.

According to the Cambridge English Dictionary, reincarnation means the belief that the soul or spirit of a dead person can return to life, not in their body, but in another body, following their death.

In Hinduism and other Indian religious traditions, reincarnation also has a spiritual element. The first reference to reincarnation is found in the Upanishads, Hindu texts that predate Buddhism and Jainism. While the idea of reincarnation differs between Hindu traditions, Hinduism generally holds that the body and the soul are different. While the physical body dies, the soul does not. The soul is indestructible.

Additionally, it should be noted that the Hindu idea of the soul is slightly different from the soul found in Western philosophies. In Western philosophies, the soul includes a person's mental abilities, including feelings, memories, thinking, etc. In Hinduism, these elements are part of a person's material self or body. Rather, the soul is the innermost self, a person's inner essence that remains unaffected by your personality and ego.

Jainism and Buddhism are similar in their ideas of the soul to Hinduism. However, in Buddhism, the soul (or atman) is not permanent, unlike in Hinduism. While there is rebirth, no permanent atman ties your lives together. Rather, there is impermanence, and everything that constitutes a being dissolves at death, after which they are reborn. In Jainism, the soul (or jiva) begins its journey in a primordial state, and as it goes through the cycles of birth and rebirth, it evolves with each rebirth.

With Hinduism, we do not think about a split afterlife. Instead, your karma affects your afterlife. You can end up in heaven if you have done good things, in hell if you have done bad, or back on Earth to grow further on your journey. As you do more good, you will become a better and better human. Furthermore, the circumstances of your future lives also depend on your karma.

However, this rebirth is not permanent—even the gods and demons die and are reborn depending on their karma. This cycle of birth, death, and rebirth continues until a person achieves the spiritual knowledge and good karma needed to attain moksha, a state of utter bliss and an escape from the reincarnation cycles.

Buddhism's tradition of rebirth is similar to Hindu traditions in that your karma affects your rebirth, and the cycle of birth, death, and rebirth is endless. In Buddhism, it is only through achieving nirvana that one can be liberated from this cycle.

In Jainism, karma holds even greater importance than in Hinduism and Buddhism. It's intricately connected to Jain philosophies, and like Buddhism and Hinduism, your karma influences your current and future lives. Additionally, some souls are thought to exist in a state of abhavya, or incapability—these souls are incapable of ever achieving moksha or liberation. A soul enters the state of abhavya after it intentionally performs an act of great evil.

Jains hold that there are four states of existence or birth categories. A person can be reborn; asdevas or demigods, manusya orhumans; tiryanca oranimals, plants and microorganisms; and naraki, which means beings of hell.

These beings live in a vertically tiered universe—the demigods at the top and beings of hell at the bottom. The better your karma, the higher on the tiers you will be reborn, and the better your circumstances will be when you are reborn. The Jain text Bhagvati sutra specifies what actions lead to what form of rebirth—violence, the killing of creatures, and eating of animals and fish lead to rebirth as a being of hell while telling lies and engaging in deception and fraud results in rebirth in the world of animals and plants. Being kind and humble results in rebirth as a human, and being austere and living a life of devotion and faithfulness to Jain tenets leads to rebirth as a demigod.

As with Hinduism and Buddhism, it's possible to be liberated from the cycle of birth and rebirth by letting go of attachments and following the fourteen stages on the path to liberation (known as Gunasthana). Some versions of Jainism hold that a soul must undergo 8,400,000 birth situations before attaining moksha. However, because we do not know where our soul is currently, we should always strive to follow the path of Gunasthana.

Sikhism's concept of karma and rebirth is relatively different from those held by the other major Indian religions. Like the other three religions, Sikhism also believes in a cycle of birth, death, and rebirth. Similarly, your karma from one life affects your circumstances in your future lives. However, your karma only influences your future lives. It's possible to attain liberation from the cycle of birth and rebirth through devotion to a god rather than a specific path to be free of attachments and gain good karma. Sikhism encourages devotion to a god to obtain mukti or liberation.

The law of karmic return has remained relatively similar across the major Indian religions. As mentioned above, the concept of reincarnation holds that the karma of your past and current lives will impact your future lives, but only at the influencing level of future lives, as in Sikhism, or determining the form of your rebirth and possibly attaining liberation from the cycle of birth and rebirth, as in Hinduism.

However, through all four major Indian religions, your karma plays a major role in your future life.

Therefore, these religions hold that performing actions that provide you with good karma is essential. The better your karma, the better your future lives will be—conversely, the worse your karma, the worse off you will be in the future, in this life, or a life in the far-off future. Every action you take will impact you, even if that impact is not immediate.

The law of karmic return is not a system of punishment and reward; rather, it is simply a law underlining the consequences of a person's actions. For example, in Jainism, a god does not influence your destiny. Instead, all your life circumstances result from your karma. This is also known as the law of cause and effect or the law of action and reaction. It essentially means that everything you put into the world, you receive back in the future, both good and bad.

How Karma Affects Your Current Life

Given the idea of reincarnation, it is easy to believe that the karma you earn in your present life will not impact your future lives. However, there are two considerations to keep in mind:

- Not all karma affects future lives—you may feel the effect of some part of your earned karma in this life.
- The karma from your past lives could be affecting your current life. So, if you consider the good and bad of your current life, keep in mind that your actions similarly affect a future reincarnation of yourself.

Understanding how karma affects your current life offers you the chance to take action to mitigate these effects or act in a way to gain "positive" karma. Here are five ways your karma is affecting your current life:

1. Since karma has no expiration date, there is a good chance that some or all of your current life events result from your soul's actions in a past life (or lives). Think of it like baggage you carry through a long trip—or, in terms of your soul, a trip through multiple reincarnations. Your bag gets heavier or lighter as you add to (take actions resulting in earning karma, negatively and positively) and subtract from it (experience the effects of past karma). You ideally want to go through life with as light a

karmic load as possible—requiring you to go through and confront your past karma. This is what karmic astrology offers.

2. No person in your life is there by coincidence. Karma means the role of everyone in your life is due to your past actions. Each is meant to teach you a specific lesson. In particular, karmic relationships will play out as planned regardless of your actions. Therefore, understanding your karma and its effect (if any) on your relationships enables you to move through this plan and start new relationships on your own terms.

3. The law of karmic return means that your actions affect your current life circumstances. However, it's essential to keep in mind that these circumstances are not only affected by your negative karma but also your positive karma. So, it's crucial to live an authentic, truthful life, enabling you to move past negative karma from a past life and start your future lives with positive karma.

4. The effect of karma often causes a reversal of roles in rebirth. For example, your parent may have been your child in a former life, while a close friend may have been someone you disliked. Even if you had a relationship with the people you know today in your respective past lives, these relationships and their impact on you might have been very different. You should approach your current relationships with the perspective that your souls are connected through lifetimes, including in future lives. Act according to how you want your future relationships with them to unfold.

5. As you have probably guessed from the above ways karma affects your current life, karma repeats through lifetimes. You know the same people and share similar relationships as you move through life. It raises several questions. Why do similar events happen through lifetimes? What should you do to break this pattern of repetition and similarity? The repetition of karma teaches you to take different actions to achieve different results. You will need to undergo true introspection and evaluate your strengths and weaknesses to determine what you can change. Change from the inside will also lead to external change, allowing you to modify and alter karma patterns. This is where karmic astrology comes in, and this modification allows

you (and future you) to live your life (or lives) your way without the burden of your past lives weighing you down.

Things You Can Do to Attract Good Karma

Are you wondering how you can attract good karma? There are numerous positive actions you can take, including:

- Practice kindness and compassion for yourself and others.
- Forgive yourself and others.
- Complement others.
- Give people good recommendations.
- Volunteer.
- Help someone find a job.
- Thank others for their help.
- Donate something valuable to a good cause (monetary or another value like your time).
- Teach someone something. It does not have to mean book learning; it could be something as simple as teaching a friend to brew a fresh cup of tea.
- Listen to others when they talk to you.
- Show up for other people.
- Reflect and introspect on your actions.

Attracting good karma essentially requires you to be kind and compassionate to others. Any actions you take that put these concepts into action will attract good karma. At the same time, avoid harming others, including non-human creatures. Harm to others attracts negative karma, and consciously avoiding it reduces your negative karma significantly, especially since the intention is a part of what earns you negative karma.

How Good Is Your Karma?

You might have taken the "How Good Is Your Karma?" quiz in the first chapter. However, now that you know more about karmic astrology and karma in general, you have likely taken steps to ensure you attract positive karma and curtail negative karma.

It would be advisable to retake the quiz as it will allow you to understand better where you currently stand and what actions you still need to take to earn further positive karma.

Answer each question truthfully and tally your results based on the instructions at the end of the quiz.

1. You find a wallet abandoned on the train. You decide to:
- a) Find the owner.
- b) Leave it where it is—someone will come and get it soon.
- c) Take out some money and return the wallet.
- d) Keep it for yourself.

2. Do you talk to homeless people?
- a) I would if I needed to
- b) Perhaps a "hi" as I walk past.
- c) I'd feel a bit nervous doing so.
- d) Never

3. You do someone a favor. Do you:
- a) Let it stay a secret—you're doing it for them, not for the acknowledgment.
- b) Let them know but downplay your efforts—you'd like a little acknowledgment but aren't interested in being the center of attention.
- c) Ensure you let the person you helped know—after all, you did it, so they would be aware that you liked them.
- d) Make sure the person you helped knows—you want to ensure they know to pay you back in the future.

4. You encounter a lost and confused tourist on the street. You:
- a) Walk with them to their destination.
- b) Offer to help with directions.
- c) Ignore them and power walk past.
- d) Point and laugh at their predicament with your friends.

5. **Do you return books from the library on time?**
    a) I return them early more often than not.
    b) I generally return them on time, but I have been late on occasion.
    c) I try returning them on time, but it's hard, and I'm generally late.
    d) I can't remember the last time I returned a library book after checking it out.

6. **Do you volunteer?**
    a) As much as I can.
    b) Occasionally, but I don't have much time to spare.
    c) I've considered it but have decided against it.
    d) Never—I have a limited time and need to focus on making money.

7. **Do you recycle?**
    a) Always.
    b) As much as possible, though I do slack off occasionally.
    c) When it's convenient.
    d) Never.

8. **Your best friend is going through a significant breakup. Do you:**
    a) Hang out with them, be there for them, and listen to them for as long as possible.
    b) Spend some time with them and take them out for a meal or two.
    c) Take them out a couple of times.
    d) Offer to split a round of drinks.

9. **Would you agree to work at a company whose mission you morally disagreed with in return for a significant salary?**
    a) No.
    b) I'd consider it, but I'd need a lot more information.
    c) I'd donate some of my paychecks, but yes.
    d) Yes.

10. Do you think people should judge others based on a single action?
- a) No.
- b) Depends on the action in question.
- c) I think judging others on their actions is justified.
- d) Yes—an illegal act should always be given the full book, regardless of personal situations

When you have finished the quiz, check your answers and list how many times you got each letter—so, how many a's, etc. The letter you get the most frequently is what you should concentrate on.

The earlier your letter, the better your karma. So, if you got more a's than other letters, you have the best possible karma. If you have more d's, you need to do some work.

Moreover, it's essential to keep in mind that even if you got all a's, you still have work to do. Do not slack off on your kindness and compassion, and work to keep attracting positive karma to lighten your existing karmic load and start your next life as much on the positive side of the column as possible.

Conclusion

Like any language, the language of karmic astrology has its own rules and style, and it takes some practice to get the hang of it. Moreover, it also includes many technical concepts like the different ideas we covered. To make the most of this knowledge, you must understand it at a deeper level and practice it frequently to see real-life results. Karmic astrology is not an answer for the rest of your life; it is a practice you can use daily to make better sense of life. By understanding how karmic astrology works out for the smaller events in your life, you can understand how reading will translate to bigger events.

Unlike palmistry and other pseudosciences, karmic astrology does not merely rely on guesswork. Throughout this book, you will have noticed that it requires a lot of highly accurate information for the reading to be precise. Even a difference in a day in the birth chart can completely change the readings. Slightly altering the time of an event can have dramatically different results. Since there are so many variables at work, it's imperative to have the most accurate information to do good readings.

You need to factor in exceptions whenever you interpret karmic astrology for yourself or someone else. There are always those Sagittarius individuals who are terrible at saving money and are extremely hyper. Even when you have done everything perfectly, you will find your results are not translating correctly. This may just be an exceptional case; it doesn't have to be a fault on your end.

While we have covered a lot of information in this book, it's always helpful to supplement your learning through other sources. There is plenty of material available on karmic astrology, and you can learn a great deal of detail on any subject of your choice. When consulting other sources, keep in mind that different practitioners have different methods of interpreting. While there is no hard and fast rule about how something can be defined, the information in this book gives you a clear direction. If you find another source with an entirely different perspective on the behavior of houses, you can be sure that you are reading from a weak information source. So, be careful when selecting the sources.

It's great to get a reading or create your own, but the main benefit of this reading is when you put it into practice. Simply writing down what you have analyzed for yourself and putting it into a drawer isn't going to help anyone. Karmic astrology aims to improve your life, which will only happen when you take action. Even if you are fearful, you need to take the first step and make a move.

Karma repeats itself; however, you have the power to change the course of your life if you truly desire it.

Here's another book by Mari Silva that you might like

Your Free Gift
(only available for a limited time)

Thanks for getting this book! If you want to learn more about various spirituality topics, then join Mari Silva's community and get a free guided meditation MP3 for awakening your third eye. This guided meditation mp3 is designed to open and strengthen ones third eye so you can experience a higher state of consciousness. Simply visit the link below the image to get started.

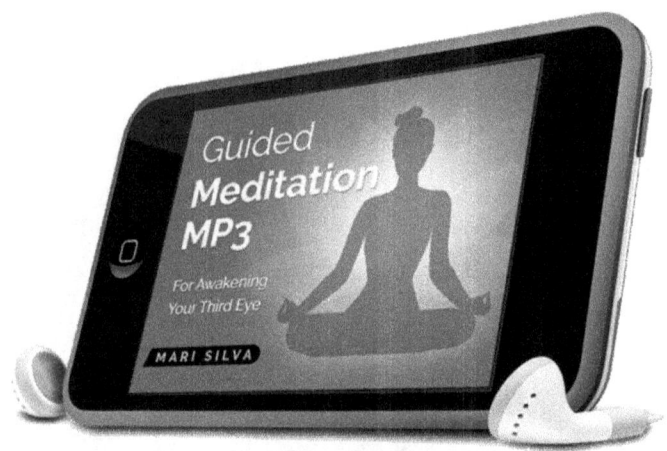

https://spiritualityspot.com/meditation

Bibliography

A, S. (2019, May 29). *Karmic astrology: Know your karma and your dharma.* WeMystic. https://www.wemystic.com/karmic-astrology/

Admin. (2013, December 12). *Karmic astrology.* ZodiacSign.com. https://www.sunsigns.org/karmic-astrology/

Allard, S. (2020, September 4). *5 things to know about karma and reincarnation.* Hindu American Foundation. https://www.hinduamerican.org/blog/5-things-to-know-about-karma-and-reincarnation

Astrology.Com. (n.d). *Birth chart calculator.* Accessed October 1, 2022. https://www.astrology.com/birth-chart/

Astrology Zodiac Signs. (n.d.). *Karmic astrology.* Astrology-Zodiac-Signs.Com. Accessed October 1, 2022. https://www.astrology-zodiac-signs.com/astrology/branches/karmic-astrology/

AstroTwins. (2020, August 31). *12 houses of the horoscope: The themes & lessons of each.* Mindbodygreen. https://www.mindbodygreen.com/articles/the-12-houses-of-astrology/

AstroTwins. (2019, June 30). *Create your free birth chart.* Astrostyle. https://astrostyle.com/birthchart/?sscid=51k6_wugvp

AstroTwins. (2019, January 31). *How to read your birth chart like an astrologer.* Mindbodygreen. https://www.mindbodygreen.com/articles/how-to-read-your-astrology-birth-chart/

Black, K. M. (n.d.). *Karmic astrology: The secret to a happy, purposeful life.* Karen M. Black. Accessed October 1, 2022. https://www.karenmblack.com/karmic-astrology.html

Black, K. M (n.d.). *Your north node soul mission: Detailed descriptions by sign and house.* Karen M. Black. Accessed October 1, 2022. https://www.karenmblack.com/north-node.html

Cafe Astrology .com. (2018, March 15). *Understanding the astrological chart wheel.* https://cafeastrology.com/articles/how-to-understand-read-chart-wheel.html

Camacho, N. A. (2022, May 18). *What the astrological house associated with your zodiac sign means for you.* Well+Good. https://www.wellandgood.com/zodiac-signs-houses/

Dasa, P. (2014, October 8). *Reincarnation and karma: How it all works.* HuffPost.

Discover Card. (2014, September 17). *How good is your karma?* BuzzFeed. https://www.buzzfeed.com/discovercard/how-good-is-your-karma

Estrada, J. (2022, June 28). *There are 12 laws of karma at play in your life—here's what they mean.* Well+Good. https://www.wellandgood.com/12-laws-of-karma/

Estrela, A. (2019, November 6). *Forecasting the future.* PsychicGuild. https://www.psychicguild.com/astrology/forecasting/

Garcia, A. (2022, March 2). *What are karmic lessons, and how we can learn from them?* AFYA AROMAS. https://shopafyaaromas.com/blogs/self-love/what-are-karmic-lessons-and-what-can-we-learn-from-them

GoldRing Astrology. (n.d.). *Reading your birth chart.* Accessed October 1, 2022. https://www.goldringastrology.com/ReadingYourBirthChart

Harra, C. (2020, February 21). *5 ways karma from your past lives affects you today.* Mindbodygreen. https://www.mindbodygreen.com/0-20223/5-ways-karma-from-your-past-lives-affects-you-today.html

Heyl, J. C. (2022, March 24). *What is a karmic cycle?* Dotdash Media. https://www.verywellmind.com/what-is-a-karmic-cycle-5219446

Hinduism Today. (2019, September 5). *Karma and reincarnation.* https://www.hinduismtoday.com/hindu-basics/karma-and-reincarnation/

Hope grows. (2020, April 24). *What is spiritual purpose?* https://hopegrows.net/news/what-is-spiritual-purpose

Kauai's Hindu Monastery. (n.d.). *Basics of Hinduism.* Accessed October 1, 2022. https://www.himalayanacademy.com/readlearn/basics/karma-reincarnation

Kelly, A. (2022, November 30). *12 zodiac signs: Dates and personality traits of each star sign.* Allure. https://www.allure.com/story/zodiac-sign-personality-traits-dates

Kelly, A. (2021, July 4). *Birth charts 101: Understanding the planets and their meanings*. Allure. https://www.allure.com/story/astrology-birth-chart-reading

Kelly, A. (2021, June 8). *What houses in your birth chart mean and how to find them*. Allure. https://www.allure.com/story/12-astrology-houses-meaning

Kent, A. E. (2015). *Astrological transits: The beginner's guide to using planetary cycles to plan and predict your day, week, year (or destiny)*. Fair Winds Press.

LaMeaux, E. C. (n.d.). *How to attract good karma*. Gaiam. https://www.gaiam.com/blogs/discover/how-to-attract-good-karma

Leek, S. (1977). *Moon signs*. W.H. Allen/Virgin Books.

Lindberg, S. (2020, November 5). *What are the 12 laws of karma?* Healthline Media. https://www.healthline.com/health/laws-of-karma

Lynsreadings.com. (n.d.). *Frequency of numbers and karmic lessons*. Accessed October 1, 2022. https://www.lynsreadings.com/karmic-lessons

Magner, E. (2022, October 4). *12 houses in astrology: Understand a new level of your zodiac sign*. Well+Good. https://www.wellandgood.com/houses-in-astrology/

Moses. (2021, March 17). *6 signs you're experiencing a karmic lesson*. PsychDigital.

Murphy, B., Jr. (2015, March 11). *10 selfless ways to build good karma and generate happiness*. Inc. Australia. https://www.inc.com/bill-murphy-jr/10-selfless-ways-to-build-good-karma-and-generate-happiness.html

Penix, S. (2018, July 9). *How the law of karmic return can help you be a better person*. Study Breaks. https://studybreaks.com/thoughts/karmic-return/

Regan, S. (2020, July 17). *How to recognize a karmic lesson & what to do about it*. Mindbodygreen. https://www.mindbodygreen.com/articles/signs-youre-receiving-a-karmic-lesson-and-what-to-do-about-it/

Regan, S. (2021, May 19). *What actually is karmic debt & how can you know if you have it?* Mindbodygreen. https://www.mindbodygreen.com/articles/karmic-debt/

Schulman, M. (1977). *Karmic astrology: v. 1*. HarperCollins Distribution Services.

Stardust, L. (2021, March 30). *How to read your birth chart*. Teen Vogue. https://www.teenvogue.com/story/how-to-read-your-birth-chart

Stinson, N. (2017, December 15). *10 ways to align with your purpose or dharma*. Chopra. https://chopra.com/articles/10-ways-to-align-with-your-purpose-or-dharma

Summit Publications. (2013, April 3). *35. The law of karmic return*.

https://www.summitlighthouse.org/inner-perspectives/karma-law-of-karmic-return/

Thomas, K. (2022, January 27). *What is a birth chart in astrology — and how do you read one?* New York Post. https://nypost.com/article/astrology-birth-chart/

TrustedTeller. (2021, December 14). *Understanding zodiac signs: Elements, qualities, and polarity.* https://trustedteller.com/blog/understanding-zodiac-signs-elements-qualities-and-polarity/

Vedanta Society of Southern California. (2016, March 14). *Karma and reincarnation.* https://vedanta.org/what-is-vedanta/karma-and-reincarnation/

Wehrstein, K. M. "Reincarnation and karma." *Psi Encyclopedia* (2021, July 7.). https://psi-encyclopedia.spr.ac.uk/articles/reincarnation-and-karma

Whitney, B. (2017, June 15). How's your karma? Zoo. https://www.zoo.com/quiz/hows-your-karma

Wright, J. (2022, March 18). *There are (at least) 9 types of astrology—which one's right for you?* PureWow. https://www.purewow.com/wellness/types-of-astrology

ZodiacPsychics.com. (n.d.). *What is karmic astrology?* Accessed October 1, 2022. https://www.zodiacpsychics.com/article/what-is-karmic-astrology.html

www.ingramcontent.com/pod-product-compliance
Lightning Source LLC
Chambersburg PA
CBHW071352160426
42811CB00095B/706